THE BIBLE FIX

**Fixing God's Word to Match the
Wisdom of Modern Man**

Ron Walser

WestBow
PRESS

Copyright © 2010 Ron Walser

All rights reserved. No part of this book may be used or reproduced by any means, graphic, electronic, or mechanical, including photocopying, recording, taping or by any information storage retrieval system without the written permission of the publisher except in the case of brief quotations embodied in critical articles and reviews.

WestBow Press books may be ordered through booksellers or by contacting:

WestBow Press
A Division of Thomas Nelson
1663 Liberty Drive
Bloomington, IN 47403
www.westbowpress.com
1-(866) 928-1240

Because of the dynamic nature of the Internet, any Web addresses or links contained in this book may have changed since publication and may no longer be valid. The views expressed in this work are solely those of the author and do not necessarily reflect the views of the publisher, and the publisher hereby disclaims any responsibility for them.

ISBN: 978-1-4497-0337-0 (sc)
ISBN: 978-1-4497-0338-7 (e)

Library of Congress Control Number: 2010931014

Cover design by: Jonathan Wahl

Printed in the United States of America

WestBow Press rev. date: 6/30/2010

Art Work Description	Source
System & Structure Puzzle pieces	Author & Clip Art
Mousetrap & Mouse	Clip Art
Anatomy of Eye	Clip Art
Money Pallet and Man Pallets of Money	http://i220.photobucket.com/albums/ dd287/loudtalker/wallstats_trillion.jpg
Train & Triangle Right Triangle	Author & Clip Art Author

Clip Art is from NOVA Development and the License Agreement paragraph 5 states:

***Use of Content:** You may use the clip art and all other content (Content) included in the software only to create presentations, publications, pages for the World Wide Web and internets and products.*

Name of Clip Art Package: ART EXPLOSION 800,000
Nova Development Corporation
23801 Calabasas Road, Suite 2005
Calabasas, CA 91302-1547
Ph: 818-591-9600
www.novadevelopment.com

CONTENTS

Introduction ix

Forward. xi
   Daddy, Where Did I Come From? xi
   State Of The Universe Address xiv
   The Battle For Our Kids. xvi
   Book's Purpose xviii
   Book Divisions. xviii

Part 1. 1
   Argument #1 1
   Argument #2 3
   Argument #3 5
   Old Testament. 9
   New Testament. 16
   Arguments #4 And #5 23
   Application Of Logic 24
   Population Growth. 24
   Gaps In The Genealogies 25
   Groaning 25
   Creation Timing. 26
   The Long Weekend 26
   Finding The Truth 27

Part 2. 29
   God Got His Science Right 29
   How Things Work In The Real World 33
   Molecular Biology 33
   Quantum Mechanics 38
   Irreducible Complexity. 41
   Biology. 42
   The Complexity Of The Eye. 44

    Vestigial Organs 46
    Mathematics. 47
    Radiometric Dating 49
    Big Bang 53
    Missing Link?. 55
    So, What's Next For You? 57

Epilogue 59
    Suggested Steps To Take 61

Appendix. 65
    Really Big Numbers 65
    Astrophysics. 67
    Light Properties 69
    Time Relativity. 73
    Quotes—Unfavorable 75
    Quotes—Favorable. 76

Introduction

By Rod Butterworth, Ph.D.

I have only known Ron Walser for three years, but during this time I have come to appreciate greatly the unique gifts that God has bestowed upon him. He came to the Lord in his forties, often considered too late and unlikely for many—especially if a person is a professed atheist and skeptic as was Ron for all those years. Since coming to the Lord Ron has diligently studied his faith, and to his delight and the appreciation of those who sit under his teaching, he has discovered that his science background in chemistry has enabled him to highlight many of the amazing evidences of supernatural design by his Creator God.

As a retired Chief Operating Officer Ron brings insight into situations by drawing parallels between the requirements for successful business and the application of biblical principles. In addition, as a member of our board of advisors for the vision of a creation museum ministry to be developed in Branson, Missouri, he has given much valuable advice and support.

Being greatly concerned with recent statistics revealing a continuing and alarming exodus of young people from the churches in which they were raised, Ron feels compelled to produce this short work to alert the Church in general to what is happening. His choice of title, *The Bible Fix,* is very appropriate, because he believes, as do I, that it is largely a departure from the absolute authority of the Bible in the lives of Christians that has brought about this situation. It is therefore only a return to accepting the truths of God's Word at face value that can help remedy what has gone wrong.

The key issue dealt with by Ron is the question of the age of the earth and the universe in which we all reside. Is the earth over four billion years old or not? If it is, then the Bible is not a supernatural book of special revelation from a Creator God. But some Christians suggest that it is possible to believe in millions of years and not be in conflict with the Bible. Known as *theistic evolution*, this idea discounts the literal reading of Genesis and the creation account as taking place in six 24-hour days approximately 6,000 years ago. Ron challenges this idea and shows its fallacies from both scripture itself and science.

It is my belief that an open minded reader of this work will be able to clearly understand the current situation and begin to see what needs to be done in the future. I heartily recommend it and pray that with the help of the ministry of the Holy Spirit many lives will be affected for good for eternity.

Forward

For some 1800 years our Christian predecessors were pleased with God's Word. Then, about 200 years ago there were some that claimed the Bible needed a "fix." According to them, modern times demanded a modern Bible and they went to work making the needed adjustments. After all, the Bible was for the most part in pretty good shape but a tweak here, a tuck over there, and it would be good for another 1800 years.

In recent years most of the changes are the results of exegetic gymnastics and have been made in an attempt to put the Bible in sync with the age of the earth as calculated by the culture. It's reasoned that if this is done correctly, the "church" can retain a sort of confidence in the divine inspiration of God's Word and at the same time, meet the "intellectual" requirements of a humanistic society. It hasn't worked. The world still hates the church and worst of all, our kids are leaving the church in droves, as the pulpit remains silent on one of the most basic questions our children are asking.

DADDY, WHERE DID I COME FROM?

Every parent knows the consequences of not answering this question truthfully and in a clear, straightforward manner. Either give your kids the honest, God-based explanation of the Bible, or they will find their own way in a smutty, dishonest world. Again, they will get answers—either from us or from the secular world.

Recently, CMOTO (Creation Museum Of The Ozarks) invited a group of creation-believing pastors to a conference-luncheon. The purpose of the affair was to expose the pastors to ways our organization can support their efforts in strengthening their creation ministries within their individual churches. A pastor that I love and pray for regularly was at the head of my list of invitees and I made certain to send out his invitation early with subsequent follow-up. The week before the conference I got an e-mail back from him explaining that he would be unable to attend. He went on to remind me that many pastors can be equally committed to the authority of Scripture but, through their exegesis of scripture, believe in an old earth.

In the case for old-earth vs. young-earth I've noticed a strange phenomena. There are those pastors who tell me that from their exegesis of the scriptures they are fully convinced that the earth is very old and their views are not in conflict with the scientific estimates. However, when I ask why they are not teaching creation using the scripture they base their view on, they tell me the subject is too divisive within their congregation and they prefer to stay clear of any discussion of it.

It seems to me that if it were too divisive, the Lord could have done a better job of skipping over the subject Himself. Instead, He refers to creation in 62 of His 66 books. (Only the short epistles of Philemon, 2 & 3 John and Jude are exempted)[1]. Being a layperson, this obvious and deliberate omission of such an important doctrine is an enigma to me.

I've never pastored a church. What I have done is run companies. Being the retired chief operating officer of a New York food company doing $40 million dollars a year, I do know something about systems,

---

1   5 Reasons to Believe in Recent Creation by Henry M. Morris III

chains of command and organizational infrastructure. If a pastor tells me that they believe in an old earth (millions of years) but don't want to teach that message from the pulpit because of controversy that will divide, I suspect something else is going on. As Christians, we are dividers.

Matthew 10:34-39 [34] *"Do not think that I have come to bring peace to the earth. I have not come to bring peace, but a sword.* [35] *For I have come to **set a man against his father**, and a **daughter against her mother**, and a **daughter-in-law against her mother-in-law**.* [36] *And a person's enemies will be those of his own household.* [37] *Whoever loves father or mother more than me is not worthy of me, and whoever loves son or daughter more than me is not worthy of me.* [38] *And whoever does not take his cross and follow me is not worthy of me.* [39] *Whoever finds his life will lose it, and whoever loses his life for my sake will find it.*

In today's society where there is so much at stake, now is not the time to be "ashamed of the gospel." In business, whenever we hire someone to fill a management position it's important to spell out his or her job description. Only through this can there be no mistake as to what's expected of them. It seems to me God is a perfect CEO and his job description for pastors was clear and concise.

> *He must hold firm to the trustworthy word as taught, so that he may be able to give instruction in sound doctrine and also to rebuke those who contradict it. Titus 1:9*

In the first chapter of Colossians, Paul speaks of the "gospel you have heard".

> *if indeed you continue in the faith, stable and steadfast, not shifting from the hope **of the gospel that you heard**, which has been proclaimed in all creation under heaven, and of which I, Paul, became a minister. **Colossians 1:23***

In the verses below, he details this gospel: 1) *Christ created everything*—**CREATION** 2) *Christ is holding all things together* *currently*—**CONSERVATION** 3) Christ has reconciled us to Him—**CONSUMMATION**.

> *[15] He is the image of the invisible God, the firstborn of all creation. [16] For by him **all things were created, in heaven and on earth, visible and invisible**, whether thrones or dominions or rulers or authorities—all things were created through him and for him. [17] And he is before all things, **and in him all things hold together**. [19] For in him all the fullness of God was pleased to dwell, [20] and through him to **reconcile** to himself all things, whether on earth or in heaven, **making peace by the blood of his cross**. Colossians 1:19-20*

These **3 C's** (**CREATION, CONSERVATION, CONSUMMATION**) make up the gospel that you and I must proclaim. In Revelation this creation gospel component is called the "**eternal gospel**".

> *Revelation 14:6-7 [6] Then I saw another angel flying directly overhead, with an **eternal gospel** to proclaim to those who dwell on earth, to every nation and tribe and language and people. [7] And he said with a loud voice, "Fear God and give him glory, because the hour of his judgment has come, and **worship him who made heaven and earth, the sea and the springs of water***

STATE OF THE UNIVERSE ADDRESS

Usually, presidents give an annual State of the Union Address to a joint session of the United States Congress. With few exceptions it begins with, "The state of the union is . . . **GOOD!**" On several occasions during creation week Creator-God saw that the **state of the universe was good**. But at the close of the 6th day, His Word declared that the **State of the Universe was Very Good!**

Today, few would doubt that the conditions have changed for the worse and now, according to scripture and just a cursory examination, the State of the Universe is **Bad**—Very Bad Indeed. In Europe, church attendance has fallen to 7%, Scandinavian to 1½%. In days past, these nations enjoyed thriving Christian churches. Today, church after church has closed their doors to worship only to reopen as nightclubs, liquor shops, and a sundry of other worldly commercial establishments. But that's over there isn't it? The wave of humanism won't come to our shores will it? Below are some quotes from a recent article that might shed some light on just how close this assault is to our shores.

> ***February 11, 2010 USA TODAY***
>
> ***Olympics fans heading to Vancouver might want to visit a vanishing cultural treasure while they're in Canada -- local churches.***
>
> *Canada has become a **"post-Christian society"** where once-dominant Anglicanism has "moved to the margins of public life," according to a bleak study reported by Michael Valpy at the* Globe and Mail.

But it gets worse.

> *A new assessment of the state of the church in Canada looks at the Anglican Diocese of British Columbia and then across the country and concludes that,*
>
>> *... at the present rate of decline -- a loss of 13,000 members per year --* ***only one Anglican would be left in Canada by 2061.***
>>
>> *... nationally, between 1961 and 2001**, the church lost 53 per cent** of its membership, declining to 642,000 from 1.36 million.* ***Between 1991 and 2001 alone, it declined by 20 per cent.***
>
> *The report zeros in on Vancouver and the adjacent Gulf Islands,* ***suggesting closing or preparing to shutter nearly two in three of its Anglican churches now that the Anglican population is***
>
>> ***...** one generation away from extinction ... The unchurched are not coming to us.*

In 2004 The Southern Baptist Convention's *Empowering Kingdom Growth* had this to say about our "state."

> "Evangelical Christianity is about to experience a train wreck if something doesn't change. Most major evangelists <u>estimate well over half of church membership is lost and 88 percent of evangelical children leave church before age 18.</u> Additionally, Barna research shows no significant statistical difference exists between those who claim to be Christians and those who do not in most categories involving belief systems and lifestyle practices.

THE BATTLE FOR OUR KIDS

He alone, who owns the youth, gains the future. No, this is not a quote from a local youth pastor at a Vacation Bible School retreat—it's from the lips of Adolph Hitler. And like Hitler, Satan has drawn the lines of battle, starting with our elementary kids and extending all the way through to the caps and gown graduation ceremonies at our colleges. When the consumer research analyst, C. Britt Beemer[2] surveyed a huge group of kids who had already left the church he found out: 1) they did not believe the Bible was relevant to their lives, 2) they began to have these doubts as early as elementary school. And the most shocking of all—kids who grew up in Sunday Schools were more inclined to have a full-fledged cultural worldview than kids who did not have Sunday School training at all!

Our approach? We change the music, seek out more youth-oriented programs, offer more field trips, etc, etc—any manmade, pragmatic scheme that comes down the pike. All of this skirts the real issue! We need to recognize right now that Satan has drawn a circle around our kids and intends to seriously diminish the next generation of believers. **We must take a stance now.** We can no longer allow the "volume" of compromise to drown out the TRUTH of scripture

---

2   From the book *Already Gone*, by Ken Ham and consumer research/analyst, C. Britt Beemer

or teach only "selective truths" that please the whole congregation. We must stop being more concerned of offending our unbelieving church attendees[3] than we are in defending the authority of God's Word. *He (Elder[4]) must hold firm to the trustworthy word as taught, so that he may be able to give instruction in sound doctrine and also to rebuke those who contradict it.* **Titus 1:9**

> I know these are "hard" words. There are times in all our lives when the words of Jesus fall on us like an unbearable weight.
>
> *John 6:60-64* [60] *When many of his disciples heard it, they said,* **"This is a hard saying; who can listen to it?"** [61] *But Jesus, knowing in himself that his disciples were grumbling about this, said to them, "Do you take offense at this?* [62] *Then what if you were to see the Son of Man ascending to where he was before?* [63] *It is the Spirit who gives life; the flesh is no help at all. The words that I have spoken to you are spirit and life.* [64] *But there are some of you who do not believe." (For Jesus knew from the beginning who those were who did not believe, and who it was who would betray him.)*

But like Peter, where else do we have to go?

> *John 6:67-68* [67] *So Jesus said to the Twelve, "Do you want to go away as well?"* [68] *Simon Peter answered him, "Lord, to whom shall we go? You have the words of eternal life,*

---

3   Lest I be misunderstood, let me say right now that I am not advocating that pastors purposely drive out unbelievers from their church—we are commanded to win lost souls to Christ. However, God's unadulterated Word must be taught and preached in the church. If it is, the believers will grow on a diet of "sheep food" and the unbelievers will eventually depart since they can only tolerate "goat food."

4   "Elder" added for clarification by the writer

BOOK'S PURPOSE

The purpose of this booklet will be to provide you with proof beyond a reasonable doubt that God created the earth, heavens and all that is in them. And that He did this in 6 literal days some 6,000 years ago. Why is the biblical creation account so important to our faith? First, MILLIONS OF YEARS is the gateway to evolution, which sets up the domino effect all the way to atheism. A point in case would be the life of Charles Darwin. He was a Bible-believing creationist when he fell in love with Charles Lyell's uniformitarianism[5]. From there, he moved from a theistic evolutionist on to being an atheist. Again, MILLIONS OF YEARS is a Trojan horse. Once it gets inside our gate, it has the ability to do great harm—all the way from weakening our faith, to turning us completely against God.

BOOK DIVISIONS

In Part 1 the age of the earth will be discussed strictly from a biblical perspective. Many times I hear pastors say with regards to the age of the earth that they just don't feel they have enough background to discuss the subject. In this area, they have the complete background from the only One who was there, the only One who truly knows how He did it. As I have said repeatedly, "the God that got His theology right is the same God that got His science right."

Part 2 is scientific observations where we can first look at the Scripture, then be able to observe God's handiwork in His Creation—WOW moments that I never tire of enjoying.

I am diligent to "study to show myself approved". However, when I stand before my Lord and Savior and He asks why I believed and taught a "young earth", I can boldly claim that's the way I understood His Word. I have incredible peace in that. For I know if

---

5 A geological doctrine that processes acting in the same manner as at present and over long spans of time are sufficient to account for all current geological features and all past geological changes. Darwin adapted this appearance of "gradualism" to his ideas evolutionism.

I am wrong and He searches my heart (which He already has), He will know that I am **sincerely wrong**. On that day, I pray for those who are found **insincerely wrong**.

Note: *All scripture quotes are English Standard Version unless otherwise noted.*

Part 1

BIBLICAL PERSPECTIVE OF A YOUNG EARTH

Below I've listed five arguments for an old earth and my responses to each one.

ARGUMENT #1

day-age theory: a compromise belief that the days of Genesis 1 are actually vast ages of different lengths, based on secular dating methods

> *Genesis 1:3-5* [3] *And God said, "Let there be light," and there was light.* [4] *And God saw that the light was good. And God separated the light from the darkness.* [5] *God called the light Day, and the darkness he called Night. And there was evening and there was morning, the first day.*

The argument is that when God used the word "day" in the verses above, as well as subsequent verses, perhaps He didn't mean an actual "day" but was referring to an "age". It would be like me saying, *"In my father's day, all cars had stick-shift transmissions."* From the context of this statement, it's easy to see that the word "day" actually means "age" or "era".

So, could the Hebrew word used here for "day", which is *yom*, actually mean an age? Dr. James Barr, perhaps the leading Hebrew scholar alive today and Regius Professor of Hebrew at Oxford University, had this to say:

> *So far as I know, there is no professor of Hebrew or Old Testament at any world-class university who does not believe that the writer(s) of Gen. 1–11 intended to convey to their readers the ideas that (a) creation took place in a series of six days which were the same as the days of 24 hours we now experience (b) the figures contained in the Genesis genealogies provided by simple addition a chronology from the beginning of the world up to later stages in the biblical story (c) Noah's Flood was understood to be worldwide and extinguish all human and animal life except for those in the ark.*

It may be important to note that Dr. Barr is not a believing Christian and does not believe the account of Genesis 1 is true. However, when it comes to translating the language, he just "calls 'em as he sees 'em."

Although you and I perhaps do not have the wherewithal to refute Dr. Barr's assessment of the translation, perhaps we can do a little digging of our own.

Throughout the Bible, *Yom*, when used with a number like first, second or third, always means a literal 24-hour day. (i.e. *And there was evening and there was morning, the **first day**.*)

> Outside Genesis 1, yom is used with a number 359 times, and each time it means an ordinary day. Why would Genesis 1 be the exception?

How about the phrase "morning and evening"?

> Outside of Genesis 1, *yom* is used with the word "evening" or "morning" 23 times and each time it means a literal 24-hour day.
>
> Outside of Genesis 1, "evening" and "morning" appear in association with one another 38 times. In all 38 instances, the reference is to a literal 24-hour day. Why should we see it differently in Genesis 1?

Let's read the scripture again. *Genesis 1:3-5* [3] *And God said, "Let there be light," and there was light.* [4] *And God saw that the light was good. And God separated the light from the darkness.* [5] *God called the light Day, and the darkness he called Night. And there was evening and there was morning, the first day.*

Does this bring to mind the old idiom? ***If it walks like a duck and quacks like a duck. . .it's a duck.***

ARGUMENT #2

gap theory: a compromise belief that a vast period of time exists between **Genesis 1:1** and **1:2** during which time the geologic eras can conveniently be placed

Genesis 1: (1) In the beginning, God created the heavens and the earth. ←-----**GAP**----→ ***(2) The earth was without form and void, and darkness was over the face of the deep. And the Spirit of God was hovering over the face of the waters.***

But here's the problem. When forcing something into a place where it doesn't belong, you cause a buckling someplace else. The same is true for scripture. Consider Exodus 20:11:

For in six days the Lord made heaven and earth, the sea, and all that is in them, and rested on the seventh day. Therefore the Lord blessed the Sabbath day and made it holy. [6] *Exodus 20:11*

---

6   God restates this again in Exodus 31:17

By introducing the millions (actually billions) of years into a gap between Genesis 1:1 and 1:2, I now need to revise Exodus 20: 11 to read:

For in one day The Lord made the earth and after allowing it to cool for 4.5 billion years, He decorated it, made the heaven, the sea, and all that is in them, and rested on the seventh day. Therefore the Lord blessed the Sabbath day and made it holy. (I like to call this the **SAV** translation—SCIENTIFICALLY ADJUSTED VERSION)

However, my adjusted scripture now runs into another problem when I encounter Proverbs 30:6. ***Do not add to his words, lest he rebuke you and you be found a liar.*** What am I to do but revise this scripture to read: ***Do not add to his words, expect if modern man has additional thoughts on the subject, lest he rebuke you and you be found a liar (SAV).***

No, when we "fix" these verses in the Bible to accommodate the current thinking of man, it causes a buckling effect all the way down the line.

However, before leaving the Gap Theory, I want to list for you the scripture that those who believe in the gap hold fast to. It is true that the writers of the books below use similar phrases found in Genesis 1:1 but look carefully at the context and you'll see they are not talking about creation.

- ***Jeremiah 4:23 I looked on the earth, and behold, it was without form and void; and to the heavens, and they had no light.*** (Here Jeremiah is not talking about judgment of the earth but of Israel—see Jeremiah 4:14, 22,31.)

- ***Isaiah 24:1 Behold, the Lord will empty the earth and make it desolate, and he will twist its surface and scatter its inhabitants.*** (In context this is a prophecy of an upcoming judgment.)

- *Isaiah 45:18 For this is what the LORD says-- he who created the heavens, he is God; he who fashioned and made the earth, he founded it; he did not create it to be empty, but formed it to be inhabited-- he says: "I am the LORD, and there is no other.* (This is a favorite verse to lift out by itself. But look at it in context with the verses before and after and it is quite clear that it refers a promise to the Israelites and a statement that the Creator-God is up to the task of delivering exactly what He says. See below.)

- *Isaiah 45:17-19 {45:17} But Israel is saved by the Lord with everlasting salvation; you shall not be put to shame or confounded to all eternity. {18} For thus says the Lord, who created the heavens (he is God!), who formed the earth and made it (he established it; he did not create it empty, he formed it to be inhabited!): "I am the Lord, and there is no other. {19} I did not speak in secret, in a land of darkness; I did not say to the offspring of Jacob, 'Seek me in vain.' I the Lord speak the truth; I declare what is right.*

ARGUMENT #3

Framework :

This is perhaps the most insidious argument of all and the favorite among most, if not all, of the modern, liberal theologians. If you can't harmonize scripture with the "scientific" age of the earth by extending each day of creation to mean millions of years (day-age theory) or you can't insert millions of years between the first two verses of Genesis (gap theory) then why not expunge the first 11 chapters of Genesis all together?

In order to accomplish this, these modern-day expositors of scripture simply declare that these 11 chapters are literary devises that only represent a rhetorical framework that expresses great spiritual themes of creation, man's fall, the worldwide flood[7], etc., but should not be taken as actual events at all. This allows them to retain a sort of confidence in the divine inspiration of God's Word and at the same time be in full "intellectual compliance" with a modern, worldly culture.

Before venturing on, I need to say just a word or two about exegesis of scripture.

> *The Protestant church, beginning with Luther, has at all times rejected this allegorizing and adhered to the safe and sane principle, practiced by Christ and the entire New Testament, namely,* **Sensum ne inferas, sed efferas:** *"Do not carry a meaning into (the Scriptures) but draw it out of (the Scriptures)".* **International Standard Bible Encyclopedia.**

In other words, if I sit down with my Bible and am already convinced from science that the earth is millions of years old, then I've "carried a meaning into the scriptures."

But what about allegories? It has been my experience that allegories in context look like. . . well, allegories. The scripture below is a good example of an allegory.

> *Isaiah 55:12 "For you shall go out in joy and be led forth in peace; the mountains and the hills before you shall break forth into singing, and all the trees of the field shall clap their hands.*

Now, compare that with:

> *Genesis 1:3-5* [3] *And God said, "Let there be light," and there was light.* [4] *And God saw that the light was good. And God separated the light from the darkness.* [5] *God called the light*

---

7   In Part 2, we will go into why modern man has denied the Flood. As you will see, this was the first step necessary to introduce the theory of Uniformitarianism.

> *Day, and the darkness he called Night. And there was evening and there was morning, the first day.*

Look at the specific, precise details in this scripture—light, day, darkness, night, evening, morning, first day. Some question why God didn't reveal to us the details of the creative process. They imply that if the scripture were historical then He would have given us more detail. Could we have understood it if He had? Not a chance. The CERN project of the Large Hadron Collider near Geneva, Switzerland serves as a strong reminder that to this day we still are incapable of understanding the simplest details of creation. This 17-mile long tunnel is intended to collide opposing particle beams of protons in the hopes of producing a speck of matter—not a universe, just a speck. This effort with its 9,000 super magnets and over 1000 of the greatest brains on the planet, are all trying to figure out how to convert energy into matter. No, we're still not ready to grasp the details of creation. What we do know is our God knows: how to do it—has done it and—now sustains it for us.

But why expunge only the first 11 chapters of Genesis? Why not draw the line at the first 12, or for that matter, why not the whole book of Genesis? Even the most liberal theologians do not doubt the historicity of Abram (Abraham) and since the narrative beginning in chapter 12 of Genesis starts with Abram, they exegete the rest of Genesis more literally. That means that starting with the Tower of Babel in chapter 11 and working backwards through Noah's Flood and finally ending back at creation, the "framework" is applied. The denial of a worldwide flood for these theologians is a further sync up with modern science that only recognizes various local floods. This scoffing at Noah's Flood is one of the Bible's most thrilling prophetic fulfillments.

> *2 Peter 3:1-7 [1] This is now the second letter that I am writing to you, beloved. In both of them I am stirring up your sincere mind by way of reminder, [2] that you should remember the predictions of the holy prophets and the commandment of the Lord and Savior through your apostles, [3] knowing this first of*

*all, that **scoffers will come in the last days** with scoffing, following their own sinful desires.* [4] *They will say, "Where is the promise of his coming? For ever since the fathers fell asleep, all things are continuing as they were from the beginning of creation."* [5] *For they deliberately overlook this fact, that the heavens existed long ago, and the earth was formed out of water and through water by the word of God,* [6] ***and that by means of these the world that then existed was deluged with water and perished.*** [7] *But by the same word the heavens and earth that now exist are stored up for fire, being kept until the day of judgment and destruction of the ungodly.*

If the framework were valid then we would not expect to see other writers of the Bible referring to the first 11 chapters of Genesis as actual events. However, again and again we see in both the Old and New Testaments alike, references to the events and people in these chapters and the writers deal with them as actual and historical persons and places.

Below is a selection of scripture from both the Old and New Testaments that recount people, places and events that are recorded in the first 11 chapters of Genesis. I realize that most of you will wish to skip over much of this scripture, giving them only a cursory scan; that's all right. Others, like me, who have a somewhat Doubting-Thomas nature and are never satisfied until "we've placed our hand in His side", will probably not be happy until they've scrutinized these verses carefully: that's also alright. I've taken the time and effort to record the following scripture because the right-view of creation is foundational to the right-view of the Bible and for that matter, the right-view of God, Jesus Christ, Holy Spirit and self. I didn't want you to have to hold this booklet in one hand while you search the scripture with the other. This view of God's Word is too important to be distracted. The translation below is from the ESV but for those who like to "drill down" deeper, I challenge you to look up these references in your own Bibles. Keep in mind that there are references to creation in 62 of the 66 books of the Bible; below is only a small selection.

OLD TESTAMENT[8]

- *Exodus 31:17 It is a sign forever between me and the people of Israel **that in six days the Lord made heaven and earth,** and on the seventh day he rested and was refreshed.'"*

- *Deuteronomy 32:7-8 [7] **Remember the days of old; consider the years of many generations**; ask your father, and he will show you, your elders, and they will tell you. [8] When the Most High gave to the nations their inheritance, when he divided mankind, he fixed the borders of the peoples according to the number of the sons of God.*

- *Joshua 24:2 And Joshua said to all the people, "Thus says the Lord, the God of Israel, '**Long ago, your fathers lived beyond the Euphrates**, Terah, the father of Abraham and of Nahor; and they served other gods.*

- *2 Kings 19:15 And Hezekiah prayed before the Lord and said: "O Lord, the God of Israel, enthroned above the cherubim, you are the God, you alone, of all the kingdoms of the earth; **you have made heaven and earth**.*

- *1 Chronicles 1:1-28 [1] **Adam**, Seth, Enosh; [2] Kenan, Mahalalel, Jared; [3] Enoch, Methuselah, Lamech; [4] Noah, Shem, Ham, and Japheth. [5] The sons of Japheth: Gomer, Magog, Madai, Javan, Tubal, Meshech, and Tiras. [6] The sons of Gomer: Ashkenaz, Riphath, and Togarmah. [7] The sons of Javan: Elishah, Tarshish, Kittim, and Rodanim. [8] The sons of Ham: Cush, Egypt, Put, and Canaan. [9] The sons of Cush: Seba, Havilah, Sabta, Raama, and Sabteca. The sons of Raamah: Sheba and Dedan. [10] Cush fathered Nimrod. He was the first on earth to be a mighty man. [11]*

---

8   The emboldened text is for emphasis and not in original translation.

Egypt fathered Ludim, Anamim, Lehabim, Naphtuhim, [12] *Pathrusim, Casluhim (from whom the Philistines came), and Caphtorim.* [13] *Canaan fathered Sidon his firstborn and Heth,* [14] *and the Jebusites, the Amorites, the Girgashites,* [15] *the Hivites, the Arkites, the Sinites,* [16] *the Arvadites, the Zemarites, and the Hamathites.* [17] *The sons of Shem: Elam, Asshur, Arpachshad, Lud, and Aram. And the sons of Aram: Uz, Hul, Gether, and Meshech.* [18] *Arpachshad fathered Shelah, and Shelah fathered Eber.* [19] *To Eber were born two sons: the name of the one was Peleg (for in his days the earth was divided), and his brother's name was Joktan.* [20] *Joktan fathered Almodad, Sheleph, Hazarmaveth, Jerah,* [21] *Hadoram, Uzal, Diklah,* [22] *Obal, Abimael, Sheba,* [23] *Ophir, Havilah, and Jobab; all these were the sons of Joktan.* [24] *Shem, Arpachshad, Shelah;* [25] *Eber, Peleg, Reu;* [26] *Serug, Nahor, Terah;* [27] *Abram, that is,* **Abraham**. [28] *The sons of Abraham: Isaac and Ishmael.*

- *Nehemiah 9:6 "You are the Lord, you alone.* **You have made heaven, the heaven of heavens, with all their host, the earth and all that is on it, the seas and all that is in them; and you preserve all of them**; *and the host of heaven worships you.*

- *Job 12:7-9* "**But ask the beasts, and they will teach you; the birds of the heavens, and they will tell you; or the bushes of the earth, and they will teach you; and the fish of the sea will declare to you. Who among all these does not know that the hand of the Lord has done this?**

- *Job 9:5-9* [5] **he who removes mountains, and they know it not, when he overturns them in his anger,** [6] **who shakes the earth out of its place, and its pillars tremble;** [7] **who commands the sun, and it does not rise; who seals up the stars;** [8] **who alone stretched** out the heavens and trampled the waves of the sea; [9] who made the Bear and Orion, the Pleiades and the chambers of the south;*

- *Job 12:15 If he withholds the waters, they dry up; if he sends them out, they overwhelm the land.*

- *Job 26:7-13* [7] *He stretches out the north over the void and hangs the earth on nothing.* [8] *He binds up the waters in his thick clouds, and the cloud is not split open under them.* [9] *He covers the face of the full moon and spreads over it his cloud.* [10] *He has inscribed a circle on the face of the waters at the boundary between light and darkness.* [11] *The pillars of heaven tremble and are astounded at his rebuke.* [12] *By his power he stilled the sea; by his understanding he shattered Rahab.* [13] *By his wind the heavens were made fair; his hand pierced the fleeing serpent.*

- *Job 38:4-7* [4] **"Where were you when I laid the foundation of the earth**? *Tell me, if you have understanding.* [5] *Who determined its measurements— surely you know! Or who stretched the line upon it?* [6] *On what were its bases sunk, or who laid its cornerstone,* [7] *when the morning stars sang together and all the sons of God shouted for joy?*

- *Psalms 33:6-9* [6] **By the word of the Lord the heavens were made**, *and by the breath of his mouth all their host.* [7] *He gathers the waters of the sea as a heap; he puts the deeps in storehouses.* [8] *Let all the earth fear the Lord; let all the inhabitants of the world stand in awe of him!* [9] *For he spoke, and it came to be; he commanded, and it stood firm.*

- *Psalms 90:2-3* [2] *Before the mountains were brought forth, or* **ever you had formed the earth and the world, from everlasting to everlasting you are God**. [3] *You return man to dust and say, "Return, O children of man!"*

- *Psalms 148:1-5* [1] *Praise the Lord! Praise the Lord from the heavens; praise him in the heights!* [2] *Praise him, all his angels; praise him, all his hosts!* [3] *Praise him, sun and moon, praise him, all you shining stars!* [4] *Praise him, you highest heavens, and you waters above the heavens!* [5] *Let them praise the name of the Lord!* **For he commanded and they were created.**

- *Psalms 29:1-11* [1] **Ascribe** *to the Lord, O heavenly beings,* **ascribe** *to the Lord glory and strength.* [2] **Ascribe** *to the Lord the glory due his name; worship the Lord in the splendor of holiness.* [3] *The* **voice of the Lord is over the water**s*; the God of glory thunders, the Lord, over many waters.* [4] *The voice of the Lord is powerful; the voice of the Lord is full of majesty.* [5] *The voice of the Lord breaks the cedars; the Lord breaks the cedars of Lebanon.* [6] *He makes Lebanon to skip like a calf, and Sirion like a young wild ox.* [7] *The voice of the Lord flashes forth flames of fire.* [8] *The voice of the Lord shakes the wilderness; the Lord shakes the wilderness of Kadesh.* [9] *The voice of the Lord makes the deer give birth and strips the forests bare, and in his temple all cry, "Glory!"* [10] *The Lord sits enthroned over the flood; the Lord sits enthroned as king forever.* [11] *May the Lord give strength to his people! May the Lord bless his people with peace!*

- *Psalms 104:1-35* [1] *Bless the Lord, O my soul! O Lord my God, you are very great! You are clothed with splendor and majesty,* [2] *covering yourself with light as with a garment,* **stretching out the heavens like a tent**. [3] *He lays the beams of his chambers on the waters; he makes the clouds his chariot; he rides on the wings of the wind;* [4] *he makes his messengers winds, his ministers a flaming fire.* [5] **He set the earth on its foundations**, *so that it should never be moved.* [6] *You covered it with the deep as with a garment; the waters stood above the mountains.* [7] *At your rebuke they fled; at the sound of your thunder they took to* flight. [8] **The mountains rose, the valleys sank down to the place that you appointed for them.** [9] You set a boundary that they may not pass, so that they might not again cover the earth. [10] You make springs gush forth in the valleys; they flow between the hills; [11] they give drink to every beast of the field; the wild donkeys quench their thirst. [12] Beside them the birds of the heavens dwell; they sing among the branches. [13] From your lofty abode you water the mountains; the earth is satisfied with the fruit of your work. [14] **You cause the grass to grow for the livestock and plants for man to cultivate, that he may bring forth food from the earth** [15] and wine to gladden the heart of man, oil to make his face shine and bread to strengthen man's heart. [16] The trees of the Lord are watered abundantly, the cedars of Lebanon that he planted. [17] In them the birds build their nests; the stork has her home in the fir trees. [18] The high mountains are for the wild goats; the rocks are a refuge for the rock badgers. [19] **He made the moon to mark the seasons; the sun knows its time for setting.** [20] You make darkness, and it is night, when all the beasts of the forest creep about. [21] The young lions roar for their prey, seeking their food from God. [22] When the sun rises, they steal away and lie down in their dens. [23] Man goes out to his work and to his labor until the evening. [24] O Lord, how manifold are your works! **In wisdom have you made them all; the earth is full of your creatures.** [25] Here is the sea, great and wide, which teems with creatures innumerable, living things both small and great. [26] There go the ships, and Leviathan, which you formed to play in it. [27] These all look to you, to give them their food in due season. [28] When you give it to them, they gather it up; when you open your hand, they are filled with good things. [29] When you hide your face, they are dismayed; when you take away their breath, they die and return to their dust. [30] When you send forth your Spirit, they are created, and you renew the face of the ground. *[31]* May the glory of the Lord endure forever; may the Lord rejoice in his works, *[32]* who looks on the earth and it trembles, who touches the mountains and they smoke! *[33]* I will sing to the Lord as long as I live; I will sing praise to my God while I have being. *[34]* May my meditation be pleasing to him, for I rejoice in the Lord. *[35]* Let sinners be consumed from the earth, and let the wicked be no more! Bless the Lord, O my soul! Praise the Lord!

- Proverbs 8:22-31 *[22]* "The Lord possessed me at the beginning of his work, the first of his acts of old. *[23]* **Ages ago I was set up, at the first, before the beginning of the earth.** *[24]* When there were no depths I was brought forth, when there were no springs abounding with water. *[25]* Before the mountains had been shaped, before the hills, I was brought forth, *[26]* **before he had made the earth with its fields, or the first of the dust of the world.** *[27]* **When he established the heavens,** I was there; when he drew a circle on the face of the deep, *[28]* when he made firm the skies above, when he established the fountains of the deep, *[29]* when he assigned to the sea its limit, so that the waters might not transgress his command, when he marked out the foundations of the earth, *[30]* then I was beside him, like a master workman, and I was daily his delight, rejoicing before him always, *[31]* rejoicing in his inhabited world and delighting in the children of man.

- Isaiah 40:26 **Lift up your eyes on high and see: who created these**? He who brings out their host by number, calling them all by name, by the greatness of his might, and because he is strong in power not one is missing.

- Isaiah 45:18 **For thus says the Lord, who created the heavens (he is God!), who formed the earth and made it (he established it; <u>he did not create it empty, he formed it to be inhabited</u>!):** "I am the Lord, and there is no other.

- *Isaiah 54:9 "**This is like the days of Noah to me**: as I swore that the waters of Noah should no more go over the earth, so I have sworn that I will not be angry with you, and will not rebuke you.*

- *Jeremiah 10:11-13* [11] *Thus shall you say to them: "The gods who did not make the heavens and the earth shall perish from the earth and from under the heavens."* [12] ***It is he who made the earth by his power, who established the world by his wisdom, and by his understanding stretched out the heavens.*** [13] *When he utters his voice, there is a tumult of waters in the heavens, and he makes the mist rise from the ends of the earth. He makes lightning for the rain, and he brings forth the wind from his storehouses.*

- *Jeremiah 31:35* **Thus says the Lord, who gives the sun for light by day and the fixed order of the moon and the stars for light by night, who stirs up the sea so that its waves roar**— *the Lord of hosts is his name:*

- *Jeremiah 51:15-16* [15] ***"It is he who made the earth by his power, who established the world by his wisdom, and by his understanding stretched out the heavens.*** [16] *When he utters his voice there is a tumult of waters in the heavens, and he makes the mist rise from the ends of the earth. He makes lightning for the rain, and he brings forth the wind from his storehouses.*

- *Ezekiel 14:14 even if these three men,* **Noah**, *Daniel, and Job, were in it, they would deliver but their own lives by their righteousness, declares the Lord God.*

- *Ezekiel 14:20 even if* **Noah**, *Daniel, and Job were in it, as I live, declares the Lord God, they would deliver neither son nor daughter. They would deliver but their own lives by their righteousness.*

- *Amos 5:8* **He who made the Pleiades and Orion, and turns deep darkness into the morning and darkens the day into night, who calls for the waters of the sea and pours them out on the surface of the earth, the Lord is his name;**

- *Amos 9:6* **who builds his upper chambers in the heavens and founds his vault upon the earth; who calls for the waters of the sea and pours them out upon the surface of the earth— the Lord is his name.**

- *Micah 5:6 they shall shepherd the land of Assyria with the sword, and the **land of Nimrod** at its entrances; and he shall deliver us from the Assyrian when he comes into our land and treads within our border.*

- *Zechariah 5:11 He said to me, "To the **land of Shinar**, to build a house for it. And when this is prepared, they will set the basket down there on its base."*

NEW TESTAMENT

- *Romans 5:12-19 [12] Therefore, just as **sin came into the world through one man**, and death through sin, and so death spread to all men because all sinned— [13] for sin indeed was in the world before the law was given, but sin is not counted where there is no law. [14] **Yet death reigned from Adam to Moses**, even over those whose sinning was not like the **transgression of Adam**, who was a type of the one who was to come. [15] But the free gift is not like the trespass. For if many died through **one man's trespass**, much more have the grace of God and the free gift by the grace of that one man Jesus Christ abounded for many. [16] And the free gift is not like the result of that **one man's sin**. For the judgment following one trespass brought condemnation, but the free gift following many trespasses brought justification. [17] For if, because of **one man's trespass**, death reigned through that one man,* *much more will those who receive the abundance of grace and the free gift of righteousness reign in life through the one man Jesus Christ.* [18] *Therefore, as one trespass led to condemnation for all men, so one act of righteousness leads to justification and life for all men.* [19] *For as by the* **one man's disobedience** *the many were made sinners, so by the one man's obedience the many will be made righteous.*

- 1 Corinthians 11:7-12 [7] *For a man ought not to cover his head, since he is the image and glory of God, but woman is the glory of man.* [8] **For man was not made from woman, but woman from man.** [9] **Neither was man created for woman, but woman for man.** [10] *That is why a wife ought to have a symbol of authority on her head, because of the angels.* [11] *Nevertheless, in the Lord woman is not independent of man nor man of woman;* [12] *for as woman was made from man, so man is now born of woman. And all things are from God.*

- 1 Corinthians 15:21-22 [21] **For as by a man came death**, *by a man has come also the resurrection of the dead.* [22] **For as in Adam all die**, *so also in Christ shall all be made alive.*

- 1 Corinthians 15:38-41 [15:38] *But God gives it a body as he has chosen,* **and to each kind of seed its own body.** [39] **For not all flesh is the same, but there is one kind for humans, another for animals, another for birds, and another for fish.** [40] *There are heavenly bodies and earthly bodies, but the glory of the heavenly is of one kind, and the glory of the earthly is of another.* [41] *There is one glory of the sun, and another glory of the moon, and another glory of the stars; for star differs from star in glory.*

- 1 Corinthians 15:45-47 [45] *Thus it is written,* "**The first man Adam became a living being**"; *the last Adam became a life-giving spirit.* [46] *But it is not the spiritual* that is first but the natural, and then the spiritual. [47] **The first man was from the earth, a man of dust**; the second man is from heaven.

- 2 Corinthians 11:3 But I am afraid that as **the serpent deceived Eve** by his cunning, your thoughts will be led astray from a sincere and pure devotion to Christ.

- 1 Timothy 2:13-15 [13] **For Adam was formed first, then Eve;** [14] **and Adam was not deceived, but the woman was deceived and became a transgressor.** [15] Yet she will be saved through childbearing—if they continue in faith and love and holiness, with self-control.

- Romans 8:18-25 [18] For I consider that the sufferings of this present time are not worth comparing with the glory that is to be revealed to us. [19] For the creation waits with eager longing for the revealing of the sons of God. [20] For the creation was subjected to futility, not willingly, but because of him who subjected it, in hope [21] that the creation itself will be set free from its bondage to corruption and obtain the freedom of the glory of the children of God. [22] **For we know that the whole creation has been groaning together in the pains of childbirth until now.** [23] And not only the creation, but we ourselves, who have the firstfruits of the Spirit, groan inwardly as we wait eagerly for adoption as sons, the redemption of our bodies. [24] For in this hope we were saved. Now hope that is seen is not hope. For who hopes for what he sees? [25] But if we hope for what we do not see, we wait for it with patience.

- Hebrews 4:1-11 [1] Therefore, while the promise of entering his rest still stands, let us fear lest any of you should seem to have failed to reach it. [2] For good news came to us just as to them, but the message they heard did not benefit them, because they were not united by faith with those who listened. [3] For we who have believed enter that rest, as he has said, "As I swore in my wrath, 'They shall not enter my rest,'" although his works were finished from the foundation of the world. [4] For he has somewhere spoken of the seventh day in this way: "**And God rested on the seventh day from all his works**." [5] And again in this passage he said, "They shall not enter my rest." [6] Since therefore it remains for some to enter it, and those who formerly received the good news failed to enter because of disobedience, [7] again he appoints a certain day, "Today," saying through David so long afterward, in the words already quoted, "Today, if you hear his voice, do not harden your hearts." [8] For if Joshua had given them rest, God would not have spoken of another day later on. [9] So then, there remains a Sabbath rest for the people of God, [10] for whoever has entered God's rest has also rested from his works as God did from his. [11] Let us therefore strive to enter that rest, so that no one may fall by the same sort of disobedience.

- Hebrews 11:1-7 [1] Now faith is the assurance of things hoped for, the conviction of things not seen. [2] For by it the people of old received their commendation. [3] **By faith we understand that the universe was created by the word of God, so that what is seen was not made out of things that are visible.** [4] **By faith Abel offered to God a more acceptable sacrifice than Cain**, through which he was commended as righteous, God commending him by accepting his gifts. And through his faith, though he died, he still speaks. [5] **By faith Enoch was taken up** so that he should not see death, and he was not found, because God had taken him. Now before he was taken he was commended as having pleased God. [6] And without faith it is impossible to please him, for whoever would draw near to God must believe that he exists and that he rewards those who seek him. [7] By faith Noah, being warned by God concerning events as yet unseen, in reverent fear constructed an ark for the saving of his household. By this he condemned the world and became an heir of the righteousness that comes by faith.

- *Hebrews 12:24 and to Jesus, the mediator of a new covenant, and to the sprinkled blood that **speaks a better word than the blood of Abel**.*

- *1 Peter 3:20 because they formerly did not obey,* ***when God's patience waited in the days of Noah, while the ark was being prepared, in which a few, that is, eight persons, were brought safely through water.***

- *2 Peter 2:4-5 {4} For if God did not spare angels when they sinned, but cast them into hell and committed them to chains of gloomy darkness to be kept until the judgment; {5} **if he did not spare the ancient world, but preserved Noah**, a herald of righteousness, with seven others, **when he brought a flood upon the world of the ungodly**;*

- *2 Peter 3:5-6 {5} **For they deliberately overlook this fact, that the heavens existed long ago, and the earth was formed out of water and through water by the word of God**, {6} **and that by means of these the world that then existed was deluged with water and perished.***

- *1 John 3:12 **We should not be like Cain**, who was of the evil one and murdered his brother. And why did he murder him? Because his own deeds were evil and his brother's righteous.*

- *Jude 1:11 Woe to them! **For they walked in the way of Cain** and abandoned themselves for the sake of gain to Balaam's error and perished in Korah's rebellion.*

- *Matthew 19:3-6 {3} And Pharisees came up to him and tested him by asking, "Is it lawful to divorce one's wife for any cause?" {4} He answered, "**Have you not read that he who created them from the beginning made them male and female**, {5} and said, 'Therefore a man shall leave his father and his mother and hold fast to his wife, and the two shall become one flesh'? {6} So they are no longer* two but one flesh. What therefore God has joined together, let not man separate."

- Mark 10:2-9 [2] And Pharisees came up and in order to test him asked, "Is it lawful for a man to divorce his wife?" [3] He answered them, "What did Moses command you?" [4] They said, "Moses allowed a man to write a certificate of divorce and to send her away." [5] And Jesus said to them, "Because of your hardness of heart he wrote you this commandment. [6] **But from the beginning of creation, 'God made them male and female.'** [7] 'Therefore a man shall leave his father and mother and hold fast to his wife, [8] and the two shall become one flesh.' So they are no longer two but one flesh. [9] What therefore God has joined together, let not man separate."

- Matthew 24:37-42 [37] **For as were the days of Noah, so will be the coming of the Son of Man.** [38] For as in those days before the flood they were eating and drinking, marrying and giving in marriage, **until the day when Noah entered the ark,** [39] **and they were unaware until the flood came and swept them all away**, so will be the coming of the Son of Man. [40] Then two men will be in the field; one will be taken and one left. [41] Two women will be grinding at the mill; one will be taken and one left. [42] Therefore, stay awake, for you do not know on what day your Lord is coming.

- Luke 17:26-27 [26] **Just as it was in the days of Noah**, so will it be in the days of the Son of Man. [27] They were eating and drinking and marrying and being given in marriage, until the day **when Noah entered the ark, and the flood came and destroyed them all.**

- Matthew 23:35 so that on you may come all the righteous blood shed on earth, **from the blood of innocent Abel to the blood of Zechariah the son of Barachiah**, whom you murdered between the sanctuary and the altar.

- Luke 11:51 **from the blood of Abel to the blood of Zechariah**, who perished between the altar and the sanctuary. Yes, I tell you, it will be required of this generation.

- Mark 13:19 For in those days there will be such tribulation as **has not been from the beginning of the creation that God created** until now, and never will be.

- John 8:44 You are of your father the devil, and your will is to do your father's desires. **He was a murderer from the beginning**, and has nothing to do with the truth, because there is no truth in him. When he lies, he speaks out of his own character, for he is a liar and the father of lies.

- Acts 7:2-4 [2] And Stephen said: "Brothers and fathers, hear me. The God of glory appeared to our father Abraham when he was in Mesopotamia, before he lived in Haran, [3] and said to him, 'Go out from your land and from your kindred and go into the land that I will show you.' [4] Then he went out from the land of the Chaldeans and lived in Haran. And after his father died, God removed him from there into this land in which you are now living.

- Acts 14:15 "Men, why are you doing these things? We also are men, of like nature with you, and we bring you good news, that you should turn from these vain things to a **living God, who made the heaven and the earth and the sea and all that is in them.**

- Acts 17:24 **The God who made the world and everything in it**, being Lord of heaven and earth, does not live in temples made by man,

- Acts 17:26 **And he made from one man every nation of mankind to live on all the face of the earth**, having determined allotted periods and the boundaries of their dwelling place,

- *Revelation 3:14 "And to the angel of the church in Laodicea write: 'The words of the Amen, the faithful and true witness,* **the beginning of God's creation.**

- *Revelation 4:11 "Worthy are you, our Lord and God, to receive glory and honor and power,* **for you created all things, and by your will they existed and were created.***"*

- *Revelation 10:6 and swore by him who lives forever and ever,* **who created heaven and what is in it, the earth and what is in it, and the sea and what is in it**, *that there would be no more delay,*

- *Revelation 14:7 And he said with a loud voice, "Fear God and give him glory, because the hour of his judgment has come, and* **worship him who made heaven and earth, the sea and the springs of water.***"*

- *John 1:1-5 [1]* **In the beginning was the Word,** *and the Word was with God, and the Word was God. [2] He was in the beginning with God. [3]* **All things were made through him, and without him was not any thing made that was made.** *[4] In him was life, and the life was the light of men. [5] The light shines in the darkness, and the darkness has not overcome it.*

ARGUMENTS #4 AND #5

There are two more arguments that are used to bring scripture into submission to the cultural worldview. They are 1) **theistic evolution** and 2) **progressive creation**. In theistic evolution, God's role is reduced to a creational "gardener" as He merely tends to the "garden" of evolution. In progressive creation, God keeps coming back at intervals over several billions of years and during each visit, promotes the species to a more complex entity. I won't go into either of these in any detail since the reader who has persevered so far knows there is no scripture to substantiate either of these views.

APPLICATION OF LOGIC

In Part 1 of this booklet, it has been my objective to present only scriptural text to support the biblical account of creation. In Part 2 you, the reader, will experience firsthand the superiority of the biblical account over man's speculative science. However, in this short, intermediate section I cannot resist listing a few logical arguments for your consideration and ask that you indulge me before we launch into Part 2.

POPULATION GROWTH

If creation week took place just 1 million years ago[9], and the population only increased by ½ % per year (current population growth rate is 2%, 4 times this amount), then the current world population living in this generation would be in excess of 10^{2100}. Since it's estimated that only 10^{130} electrons could be squeezed into the entire known universe, 10^{2100} is a bit absurd. Even trying to make adjustments, using ridiculously low annual population growth percentages, can't get us to the current population figure of 6.5^9 (6.5 Billion). It should be noted that by using the population growth rate of ½% per year, a little over 4,500 years[10] gets us pretty close to today's world population[11]. There will be much more about young-earth calculations in the science portion of this booklet.

---

9 Scientific Creationism by Henry M. Morris, page 167

10 This number agrees with the approximate date of the Great Flood

11 Scholars place Noah's Flood at about 2500 B.C. or approximately 4,500 years ago.

GAPS IN THE GENEALOGIES

There are 20 patriarchs listed in the Bible between Adam and Abram (Abraham). For most scholars, these 20 patriarchs cover a span of time of some 2,000 years. That means that the average lifespan for them was 100 years[12]. If we believe that God created Adam "in the beginning" and we try to mesh that with a 4.7 billion year old earth, we get some silly math. Since it's easy, I'll use an assumed 4 billion as the number of years between Adam and Abram. That means either 1) each of the patriarchs had to have an average lifespan of 200 million years[13] or 2) God chose to only tell us about 20 of the patriarchs but left out of his history 40 million[14] of our forefathers that did nothing worthy of mention.

Of course all this is all a moot point indeed, since if we had 4 billion years of procreation, our current generation would "outnumber the stars" –literally.

GROANING

Theistic evolution believes in a system where death and destruction provides a benign environment where all things, matter and species, are gradually improved. The biblical account records that since the Fall, and the entrance of sin into the world, we are spiraling down, not upward. Paul states this very well in his letter to the Romans: ***For we know that the whole creation has been groaning together in the pains of childbirth until now.*** Romans 8:22

The Second Law of Thermodynamics is one of the most revered scientific principles of our times. This law states that in an isolated system that is not in a state of equilibrium, entropy will increase. In this way, increased entropy in a system is a measure of the system's disorder and thus the description: ***things go from order to disorder.*** That's why from the time a system (the universe is a system) is born it

---

12 2,000 years / 20 patriarchs = 100 year lifespan

13 4,000,000,000 years / 20 patriarchs = 200,000,000

14 4,000,000,000 years / 100 yr lifespan of new patriarchs = 40,000,000 new patriarchs

starts to wind down and wear out. ***Lift up your eyes to the heavens, and look at the earth beneath; for the heavens vanish like smoke, <u>the earth will wear out like a garment</u>, and they who dwell in it will die in like manner; but my salvation will be forever, and my righteousness will never be dismayed. Isaiah 51:6***

CREATION TIMING

Those that would apply the "day-age"[15] theory to the biblical creation account encounter a serious logical hurdle with creation timing. If God made the plants on day 3 and the sun and moon on day 4, and if there were huge gaps of time between these day-age periods, then He would have "marooned" the plants on an earth that would not supply them the needed energy source to survive. The plants are marvelous mechanisms of energy conversion using a process known as photosynthesis. Using this method these small "factories" convert the random, unusable energy from the sun, into a usable energy source to fire not only their cells, but are the sole supply of energy for the cells of every living creature on the earth[16]. It seems illogical to me that if the "day-age" theory were true, God would not have organized His work schedule in this particular sequence.

THE LONG WEEKEND

> *Exodus 20:8-11* [20:8] *"Remember the Sabbath day, to keep it holy.* [9] *Six days you shall labor, and do all your work,* [10] *but the seventh day is a Sabbath to the Lord your God. On it you shall not do any work, you, or your son, or your daughter, your male servant, or your female servant, or your livestock, or the sojourner who is within your gates.* [11] *For in six days the Lord made heaven and earth, the sea, and all that is in them,*

---

15   The theory where each day listed in the creation account of Genesis, is not a literal 24-hour day but represents millions, perhaps billions, of years.

16   For us, the fuel of life comes from either the plants themselves or from animals that have eaten the plants. Either way, you and I are inexplicably linked to the process of photosynthesis.

and rested on the seventh day. Therefore the Lord blessed the Sabbath day and made it holy.

From the context of the above scripture, the cleanest and most straightforward interpretation of the text is that God is commanding the Israelites to observe the seventh day as the Sabbath just as He had done during creation week. If each of the days during His week of creation represented millions of years (day-age theory) then I can only assume that the seventh day would also be a million years long. It seems to me this million-year Sabbath would provide an unrealistic long weekend!

FINDING THE TRUTH

There are many good commentaries—I use them regularly. However, I never confuse what God says in His Word with what another person says He says. 2 Timothy 2:15 *Do your best to present yourself to God as one approved, a worker who has no need to be ashamed, rightly handling the word of truth.* Before buying completely what another man says about the first 11 chapters of Genesis, I suggest you be in both prayer and diligent study of God's Word to determine the TRUTH for yourself.

If you believe that God created all things using an evolutionary mechanism over billions of years, you did not arrive at this conclusion by pouring over the pages of His Holy Word.

Part 2

SCIENCE PERSPECTIVE

GOD GOT HIS SCIENCE RIGHT

> *1 Peter 3:15 but in your hearts honor Christ the Lord as holy, always being prepared to make a defense to anyone who asks you for a reason for the hope that is in you; yet do it with gentleness and respect,*

God has never asked us to accept His Word without having good reason. Although belief in Christ is a matter of faith, the Bible has gone to great lengths to provide us with information that would lead us to, and strengthen the faith, that we already have. I lived much of my adult life as an unbeliever and used science as my crutch of disbelief. My attitude towards God was that if He would just show me scientifically how He had accomplished what He claimed, I would believe. God seemed to answer that if I were to believe first, then He would show me. Since becoming a believer I can't help but see God's "fingerprints" everywhere I look in science. Many of you will not share my view of God's scientific intervention with the same zeal that I have, and that's all right. Perhaps there are other ways you see God's evidence in your life. I hope that one or more of the ministries of the Holy Spirit resonate in your everyday life and serve to consume you with an equal passion. The key is that regardless of what prepares you to give your reason, hold it as a treasure in your heart and continue to "water" it daily since: *So we do not lose heart. Though our outer self is wasting away, <u>our inner self is being renewed day by day</u>. 2 Corinthians 4:16*

In a court of law, they only call eyewitnesses to the stand. Anything short of this and your testimony is invalid. We are called to be eyewitnesses for Jesus and therefore, whether it comes from His work in our lives or us seeing His hand in all creation, many times it is both, we must be prepared to share these issues with conviction.

In Part 2 of this booklet, I have compared scientific beliefs and philosophies (what science calls theories) with scripture. Scientists like to refer to sciences like mathematics and chemistry as being an observational science. In math, two plus two is always four; the Pythagorean theorem always works. (In a right triangle, the square of the hypotenuse is always equal to the sum of the square of the other two sides.) In chemistry, if you mix the same ingredients in the same proportion, temperature and pressure, you always get the same result. All scientific disciplines have much of their concentration centered on observation. However, when good science strays from what is observable and into historical conjecture, then the output of these results must carry an entirely different weight. The conclusions drawn from conjecture can, and often are, shaped by ideology, prejudice, peer pressure and financial need. I have no problem with observational sciences. But what about the other?—the historical sciences, the ideas and concepts that in reality are merely philosophies. The question arises: should they be taught to our children and grandchildren as if they were facts? Good science demands that: 1) we have total objectivity or as it's usually viewed, the rejection of all previous authority[17] and 2) access to experimentation in order to

---

17 Try as we may, we all filter reality through a set of presuppositions. In this sense, objectivity becomes tainted with a certain amount of subjectivity.

substantiate a theory. The historical portions of such sciences such as cosmology, anthropology, geology and paleontology[18] do not meet all of these criteria. If an individual, or group of individuals, receives a grant to find the "missing link", they had better find something. If there is no find, their funding is cut off and the sought after recognition and approval by their colleagues is never realized. So they start out their search with a prejudgment —sort of like shooting the arrow first and then drawing the bull's eye wherever the arrow lands. Next, if they claim that their drawn conclusions come from "assumed" events that took place millions of years ago, then it's impossible to have access to any experimentation that could either prove or disprove their philosophy. As an example, let's consider the following facts and conclusions of a hypothetical scientific group, fully financed by a grant, and searching for the "missing link."

> *The ABC Exploration Group discovers an ancient campsite. In evidence are the remnants of crude hand tools, a sure sign of intelligent life forms. Nearby they discover the burial ground. The skulls found therein are definitely not human; in fact, they resemble today's chimpanzee. Wow—what a discovery! They write their papers, present their evidence to the Academy of Sciences, and are heralded as having made one of the truly great discoveries of our century. Future grant money is guaranteed and everybody lives happily ever after—or do they?*
>
> **Let me give you my spin observing the same "facts".**
>
> *A group of traveling nomads in the past occupied the site uncovered by our exploration group. These nomads lived on a diet that included chimpanzees. As a group, they savored this delicacy on an occasional basis and when they were done with the bones of their dinners, they discarded them just outside their camp. Being nomads, they never stayed in one place too long and so after a time, they picked up and moved, leaving behind a stray tool or broken bit of pottery. Can I prove my spin? Can I subject it to experimentation in order to substantiate it? No,*

---

18 Portions of these fields can be considered as "good" science. My referral here is to the areas that are totally speculative in nature.

> *but neither can our group of scientists. We're all speculating, all developing philosophies, but none of it is true-science.* ***The major difference in our two spins is that I can't get any funding for my observations.***

In Part 2 we will have an opportunity to explore several of these "scientific myths" that are being thrust upon our current-day schoolchildren as if they were absolute, etched-in-stone, facts. Furthermore, Christians have been outmaneuvered in this arena since the only approved method of teaching science in the public school is that of naturalism which is the belief that all things must develop on their own and without the influence of a supernatural force. In looking at this material, I believe that you will concur with me that as pure science, the Christian's interpretations are better reasoning than that which is being taught to our children. In the book of Daniel, the angel tells Daniel, *But you, Daniel, close up and seal the words of the scroll until the time of the end. Many will go here and there to increase knowledge."* In science, man has gone here and there and knowledge (information) has increased. As Christians, we must also keep up with this information and test it against God's Word and in the long run, be prepared to give a reason for our faith. Jesus said, "render unto Caesar what is Caesar's' and unto God, what is God's." If the worldly system is intent on teaching a creation without God, we must pick up the banner and teach our own children the TRUTH. Do not be dismayed that the world has worked hard to capture the minds of young Christians. After all, Jesus warned us... **Luke 16:8 *The master commended the dishonest manager for his shrewdness. For the sons of this world are more shrewd in dealing with their own generation than the sons of light.***

And again. . .

> *1 Timothy 6:20-21 [20] (ESV) O Timothy, guard the deposit entrusted to you. Avoid the irreverent* **babble** *and contradictions of what* **is falsely called "knowledge**,*" [21] for by professing it some have swerved from the faith. Grace be with you.*

HOW THINGS WORK IN THE REAL WORLD

When I was a kid there was a story where a lovely young princess kissed a frog and he turned into a handsome prince. As I got older the story was embellished. In high school and college I found out that a molecule turned into a handsome frog, then into a prince, and all this without the aid of a princess' kiss. What a great bedtime story but alas, it doesn't work that way in the real world.

MOLECULAR BIOLOGY

What is information? The Merriam-Webster Dictionary defines it as: (1a) the communication or reception of knowledge or intelligence. However, this is not the definition of information that impacts molecular biology. The definition that we want to discuss here is: (2b): the ***attribute inherent in and communicated by one of two or more alternative sequences or arrangements of something (as nucleotides in DNA or binary digits in a computer program) that produce specific effects.*** That is, "**text or instructions that produce a specific effect.**" Perhaps the best way to explain this kind of information is to relate the following apologue that was used in a popular book[19].

> *The huge "ears" of SETI (Search for Extraterrestrial Intelligent) receive the long awaited signal from outer space that gives them final proof that there is intelligent life somewhere besides planet earth. Can you envision the excitement as the scientists decode a sequence of various bleeps and buzzes contained in a contiguous string of radio broadcasts? These sequences, not unlike the dots and dashes of our very own Morse code, are carefully arranged so there can be no doubt—there is intelligence required in this specific and organized arrangement of tones. And then the encoded message is read for the first time. . .* **For God so loved the world, that he gave his only Son, that whoever believes in him should not perish but have eternal life.**

19　SHOW ME GOD by Fred Heeren

This is what the Merriam-Webster means when it says a sequence of arrangements that produce specific effects. The information contained in our DNA is just this. It is an arrangement of specific informational bits that communicate instructions for all of the cell's repair and replacement activities. The operative word is "specific". Instructions cannot come from a random, non-goal oriented process, but must be developed and put into use by intelligence and in this case, intelligence beyond human comprehension.

Going one level deeper provides even greater awe of our Creator as we begin to understand how the information of the DNA gets "read" so its instructions can be acted upon. In any transfer of data in an informational system, two devices are required. The TRANSCRIBER and the READER (or Translator). Again I would ask that you, the reader, use your imagination by envisioning a DVD that contains your favorite movie. As I present it to you, you sadly inform me that you do not own a DVD player. However, you don't need to worry since I've included instructions on this DVD explaining how to make a DVD player. I proudly give it to you only to see that you are now completely dumbfounded. The unsolvable conundrum of course is: that for you to create a DVD player, you need to play the DVD so that you can get the instructions on how to build the player[20]—a modern day version of "which came first; the chicken or the egg" and what scientists refer to as a causality dilemma[21].

This is exactly what happens at the cellular level. Information is copied from the DNA double helix structure (a process known as transcription) and transported by intracellular transport

---

20 This DVD analogy was used at the January 28, 2010 CMOTO Pastors' Conference by Fred H. Groves, Ph.D.- Professor and Department Head – Reading, Foundations, & Technology – College of Education – Missouri State University

21 Causality dilemma—Scientists like a straightforward Cause and Effect. When they see an Effect, they look for a simple link to the Cause. When they cannot determine the Cause, it's called a "causality dilemma".

mechanisms[22] until they reach the cell's ribosome (a cellular factory). It is here that the transcribed information is read (translated). The ribosome is equivalent to the DVD player in our previous example and the instructions for how to build the ribosome are encoded in the DNA "database". You can't have a reader until it's built—and to build a reader you must be able to "read" the instructions.

Here's the important thing to take away from all of this. The Merriam-Webster's 2 (b) definition for "information" is: *the attribute inherent in and communicated by one of two or more alternative sequences or arrangements of something (as nucleotides in DNA or binary digits in a computer program) that produce specific effects.* When we see an orderly arrangement, in sequence, of anything, that produces a specific effect, we know there is INTELLIGENCE at its source. A Morse Code-like message from outer space quoting John 3:16 is proof that INTELLIGENCE is behind the message. (The scientific principle behind SETI is DDM, Design Detection Methodology) When we see information within our cells being used to create a specific effect, we know at its source is INTELLIGENCE. Does this bring to mind: *For you formed my inward parts; you knitted me together in my mother's womb. I praise you, for I am fearfully and wonderfully made. Wonderful are your works; my soul knows it very well. Psalms 139:13-14*

When Charles Darwin wrote *Origins of Species* in 1859, many of sciences' discoveries still lay in the future. To Darwin, the human cells were simply blobs of nondescript matter that he could imagine would somehow gradually upgrade themselves by random chance, and improve in function until they were part of a more complex mechanism. It would be 73 years before the electron microscope would show up and we would have to wait until the mid-1950's before science would even have a clue as to how complicated

---

22 For brevity, this very complex discussion has been greatly simplified. For readers wanting more information on how these nanomachines are tagged and allowed to travel within the cell itself, I suggest you google the words "intracellular transport" on the Internet.

the body is at the molecular level. Today, nearly 150 years after Darwin's book was published, the ballgame has changed. Modern science has discovered that the "blobs" of Darwin's conjecture have turned out to be extremely complicated devices, driven by an internal sophisticated information processing system. Each of the Darwinian "blobs", the human cell, contains an estimated 1.5 gigabytes of encoded information from the DNA[23] and there is an estimated 100 trillion cells in the human body. Richard Dawkins, the crown prince of atheism, admits, *"There is enough information capacity in a single human cell to store the Encyclopedia Britannica, all 30 volumes of it, three or four times over."*[24] Unlike any informational storage device made by man, the storage potential of the DNA is so dense that if one were to type out the amount of information that could be stored in a single pinhead, it would fill enough paperback books to reach from the earth to the moon 500 times[25].

The cells in the human body are in constant need of repair and replacement. The cells lining the intestines are replaced every two to three days (faster if you eat hot, spicy foods), the cells of the entire skin every two weeks and the skeletal structure every seven years[26]. The amazing informational system of the DNA provides the "intelligence" to function as a cellular "general contractor", overseeing the repair and replacement of these cells as if it were a 100-trillion-room-building and it does this again and again for almost one hundred years without ever breaking a sweat.

When Lindberg flew the Atlantic, the then president of General Motors threw down that day's newspaper in front of his staff and announced, "There's something you can't do with a committee." I would truly pay "good money" to see a committee try to assemble a single protein, yet alone handle the body's replacement needs for one day.

---

23 http://www.scripps.edu/mb/goodsell/pdb/pdb23/pdb23_1.html
24 Dawkins, R., *The Blind Watchmaker*, W.W. Norton, NY, USA, p. 115, 1986.
25 Gitt W., **Dazzling design in miniature**, *Creation* **20**(1):6, 1997.
26 Richard A. Swenson, M.D. *More Than Meet the Eye* NAVPRESS 2000 p. 20

The evidence that we see from this system of cell replacement and repair is incredible. In all normal systems scientist look for structure and order. Further more, structure and order requires information, complexity, organization and integration. When we start with the Bible and then look to the evidence, we see the support for God's Word. When we read, "I am fearfully made and You knitted me together", then look at the system of the cell, we encounter information, complexity, organization and integration—evidence that supports the scripture. On the other hand, if we believe in the non-goal oriented, random process of evolution, we would expect to see this random process being played out at the cellular level. We don't.

Again, it is not the purpose of this booklet to "prove" God created all things as He claims to have in His Word—that is an issue of faith and faith alone. However, the best scientific model for origins is that which is explained by the Hebrew God—our Lord and Savior.

QUANTUM MECHANICS

I've purposely put the above discussion of molecular biology before quantum mechanics for a reason. It's true that in the sequence of events, atoms (our discussion of quantum mechanics) must first be in place before you can even get cells or for that matter, DNA itself. However, if the system of information isn't in place before we get molecules, then all things stop in their tracks. Let me give you a real life story. Stanley Miller, a PhD who earned his doctorate in chemistry at University of Chicago, conducted the now-famous Miller-Urey experiment where he set out to "create" life in a test tube. It was his goal to show that it could be done without the aid of an intelligent agent and thus prove that spontaneous origin of life was possible. After much preparation, using his best intelligence and trial and error attempts, he finally was able to produce a few amino acids. However, these amino acids (amino acids function as building blocks for proteins) just lay in their test tube, unable to proceed without instructions from an informational system.

Here we are at another conundrum. We need some of God's basic building blocks, the chemical elements[27], to construct the molecules that make up the DNA, but the instructions to make these amino acids, reside in the informational system of the DNA itself: no DNA, no elements; and no elements, no DNA. Let me think just a moment. Wait, I've got it! Both DNA and elements have to be brought into existence simultaneously (*ex nihilo*[28]) by God the Creator.

Before getting into the good stuff about matter and energy, we need to bring up the issue of "free lunch". All, and I mean all, evolutionary theory demands a liberal, "free lunch" mindset. That is, evolution requires that certain laws of physics be in place and

---

27 Everything we know is made up of the "building blocks" of creation. There are currently 117 different chemical elements list on the Chemical Periodic Table. If we bring back rocks from the moon, God used these same building blocks there.

28 ex nihilo—Latin phrase meaning *"out of nothing"*.

provide a readymade foundation for any of its, regardless as to the question of how these laws came into being. There's an old maxim that scientists like to joke about, that best illustrates this story.

> *An accomplished scientist bragged to God that he was certain he could produce life in much the same way as God had. God challenged him to a showdown and so at the proper time and place, a crowd gathered to see man go head-to-head with God. The crowd went silent as the scientist began to rake in huge quantities of dirt with his bare hands. Again and again he reached out and pulled the dirt into himself and as the crowd looked on, a rough shape of a man started to take place. The scientist took in a deep breath, bent over his neat pile of dirt and was just about to exhale into it when a booming voice said, "S T O P !" The scientist breathed out, pulled back and answered, "What is it, God?" Then as the crowd listened intently, God answered the scientist, "GET YOUR OWN DIRT."*

You and I were born into a world where gravity, matter, informational systems and electromagnetic attraction between subatomic particles were already in place and functional. We don't know how they work or how to make them. If we base a hypothesis of origins using one or more of these unknowns, then we must be prepared to explain them also. We cannot skip over this part of our explanation: in science, there can be no "free lunch." I've always said that producing a man from an ape would be a good trick, but producing a molecule from nothing? That would be in a class all by itself. I think as you proceed in this booklet you will appreciate "ex nihilo": God creating things out of nothing, as the most scientific wonder we will discuss.

So, how do you make something from nothing? If frogs and men can't be brought into being by kisses, then how? The Bible says, *In the beginning was the Word, and the Word was with God, and the Word was God. He was with God in the beginning. Through Him all things were made; without Him nothing was made that has been made. (John 1:1-3)* Therefore, the Word (Jesus) created it all. What did he actually create? What were the building blocks of all His creation? All things that were made were made from atoms—tiny invisible particles consisting of a nucleus (protons & neutrons) with tiny little satellites (electrons) whirling around the much larger nucleus – so far, so good. It seems like I've seen this arrangement in nature somewhere else—something larger, something I wouldn't have to squint to see. I know … the universe. With all its stars and the myriad of satellites rotating around and around their nuclei, they act just like the building blocks of all creation. It would have been nice if God had given us a clue to this plan. That way we could have seen His "fingerprints" on the things He touched.

Oops! I just found it.

> ***Psalms 19:1** The heavens declare the glory of God, and the sky above proclaims his handiwork.*
>
> ***Romans 1:20** For his invisible attributes, namely, his eternal power and divine nature, have been clearly perceived, ever since the creation of the world, in the things that have been made. So they are without excuse.*

But I have a question. If these tiny little atoms are made up of larger nuclei with much smaller electrons revolving around them, what keeps the electrons from either flying off into space (because of velocity) or falling into the protons/neutrons (because of mass difference)? Aha, science has the answer. They say that there are pairs of quarks and antiquarks that form a meson and the meson, in turn, resides with the nucleus and solves all this potential disaster by holding everything together like some kind of adhesive. There, don't you feel relieved? There is a slight problem—they've never seen them. They aren't in full agreement that this mechanism exists at all but think they must be there since what else could be holding these things together like some super glue for atoms. I think that the best person to worry about how they should be held together is the one who put them together in the first place—Jesus Christ. What does the Bible have to say about keeping these atoms intact?

He is the image of the invisible God, the firstborn over all creation. For by him all things were created: things in heaven and on earth, visible and invisible, whether thrones or powers or rulers or authorities; all things were created by him and for him. **He is before all things, and in him all things hold together.** *Col 1:15-17 (NIV)*

Well, I feel better now knowing Jesus has been holding all these little atoms together ever since He made them. No need to worry; or is there? *But the day of the Lord will come as a thief in the night; in which the heavens shall pass away with a great noise, and the* **elements** *shall melt with fervent heat, the earth also and the works that are therein shall be burned up. 2 Peter 3:10 (KJV)* This could be a problem. Peter has said that the "elements" will melt from fervent heat. To do this, all Jesus has to do is release His Godly Super Glue on the atoms and we'll have a fireworks display that will make the bombs of Hiroshima and Nagasaki look like a 4th of July ice cream social.

Let's recap our discussion on quantum mechanics. Jesus Christ, the creative agent of the Godhead Trinity, created all the atoms of the universe. Up to now, He has continued to hold them together through His power and grace and when the time is right, He will release them to burn up so that we, the believers in Christ, can start with everything brand new again. God is not in the renovation business. He said He would give us a new heart and a New Jerusalem – everything new; nothing will be repaired or renovated. Why? He can't use the old. It's cursed. He did that at the time Adam fell. You and I can look forward to a new creation to match our new spirit. What a glorious God we have.

IRREDUCIBLE COMPLEXITY

Since the cells are irreducibly complex (all the parts are required), many top biochemists are recognizing that the cell could not have developed piece-meal as required by evolution. See the example of IRREDUCIBLE COMPLEXITY[29] on the next page.

---

29 An expression used by Michael Behe in his book, DARWIN'S BLACK BOX

In the illustration above, the mousetrap is said to be irreducibly complex since you cannot remove one single element of the device and still have a working mousetrap.

The mousetrap contains 5 elements to make it funcitonal: 1) Platform 2) Spring 3) Hammer 4) Holding Bar 5) Catch

In the same way, the trap cannot have had any function while waiting for one of the elements to evolve. Just as it's true with traps, cassette tape players cannot evolve into CD systems—the different machines require different, functional elements.

During our lessons, much more detail will be covered relative to this *invisible* world.

BIOLOGY

But, what about evolution—maybe Jesus did create the atoms and does hold them together, but couldn't one species evolve into another? Let's see what God has to say on the subject. *So God created the great creatures of the sea and every living and moving thing with which the water teems, according to their kinds, and every winged bird according to its kind. And God saw that it was good. God made the wild animals according to their kinds, the livestock according to their kinds, and all the creatures that move along the ground according to their kinds. And God saw that it was good." (Genesis 1:21 & 1:25)* Gee whiz, why does God have to be so fussy on this one? You'd think that just maybe He'd cut us a little slack on this "kinds" business. The DNA does demonstrate incredible flexibility with its ability to produce a wide range of dogs with various sizing, shapes and fur covering. However, they're all dogs. The same is true with cattle, racehorses and humans. Regardless of the variety that can be produced, we cannot cross the "kinds" barrier.

But aren't animal forms changing all the time right before our eyes? Isn't the process observable? NO! —Not now, not ever. Poor old Darwin had to say, "Not one change of species into another is on record ... we cannot prove that a single species has been changed"[30]. What is cited as being a form of evolution is nothing more than natural selection[31]. As an example, take the peppered moth (Biston betularia) of England. During the period of the industrial revolution, an evolutionist, Dr. Bernard Kettleworth at Oxford, claimed that the gene pool was being skewed resulting in a decreased number of the lighter colored moths. He drew the conclusion that the industrial smoke was darkening the trees and from this, the darker trees made the lighter colored moths more visible to hungry birds and therefore there was a reduction in their numbers. The result of his paper was widely published as evidence of evolution. In actuality, it was moths turning into more moths.

Natural selection is to be expected. It would be no different if we took red, white and blue bunnies to the Arctic and turned them loose. In a short period of time we would find that the rabbits' natural predators could readily see the red and blue bunnies on the white snow and their days would be numbered. In this case, if you were red or blue, you wouldn't be around long enough to do much breeding and so the gene pool becomes dominated by white bunnies.

---

30 Darwin, Francis—*The Life and Letters of Charles Darwin*, Vol 1, p. 210
31 Natural Selection def from Merriam-Webster: *a natural process that results in the survival and reproductive success of individuals or groups best adjusted to their environment and that leads to the perpetuation of genetic qualities best suited to that particular environment*

But supposing the red and blue bunnies decided that if they could develop wings and the ability to fly, many of their species could escape capture. So, after several generations and a lot of careful and selective breeding, they find that they can develop one wing. But one wing won't get you airborne. In fact, it's a handicap. You can't run as fast, you can't get in as tight a hole and it turns out to be a downward vertical change in species that serves no purpose. This is the way for all examples of piece-meal, non-goal oriented evolution. Unless a new kind of rabbit can be born with two wings, fully functional, the chance of changing the gene pool is nonexistent. No animal can mutate for generation after generation until finally evolving into a species with superior capabilities. This is what the evolutionists refer to as a vertical change in the species. This is supposed to be accomplished by accident with no engineered plan or forethought. As Darwin said, this has never been observed. Within species, we do see horizontal changes due to the incredible versatility of the DNA. Michael Jordan and I are both men. My shoe size is a 10 and his, an 18. I'm 5'10", he's ... well, taller than I am. (I have slightly more hair. . . I think.) I have a Miniature Poodle—a friend of mine has a Great Dane—both dogs, but very different. Within this tremendous versatility of the DNA, we can create a huge variety, but they're all after their own kind and all varieties are horizontal in nature, never vertical[32]. Isn't it just like a loving God to put in place a mechanism that would allow each of us to be unique?

THE COMPLEXITY OF THE EYE

Our eyes are one of the great wonders of the universe. They have the ability to focus for various depths of field, adjust an aperture for degrees of light ranging from almost complete darkness to bright sunlight, and then capture an image through a complicated arrangement of lens. These electrochemical impulses are then transmitted upside down to the visual cortex of our brain and interpreted for recognition. They do all this repeatedly each day with no complaining. Piece-meal development of this incredible organ makes no sense whatsoever. The only eye that can be of benefit is a fully functioning eye. The belief that the eye could

---

32   Mutations don't produce a net increase in genetic information—they lose information.

have developed in stages (required by piece-meal evolutionists) defies even the most vivid imagination. But don't take my word for it, Darwin was much more eloquent on the matter. "To suppose the eye, with its inimitable contrivances for adjusting the focus to different distances, for admitting different amounts of light, and for the correction of spherical and chromatic aberrations, could have been formed by natural selection, seems, I freely confess, absurd in the highest possible degree. The belief that an organ as perfect as the eye could have formed by natural selection is more than enough to stagger anyone."[33] Let's allow Darwin to rest our case on piece-meal evolution.

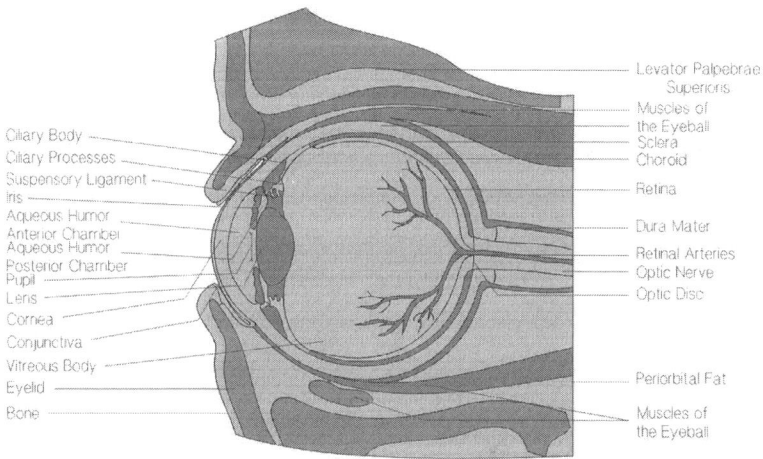

Look at the diagram of a working eye (above). Does this look like a structure that could come into being without planning and through a random, piece-meal assembly? Isn't it more likely that you could get a brand new ROLEX wristwatch (a much simpler device) by putting a bunch of scrap metal in your drawer and waiting for eons while it turned into a ROLEX?

---

33 Darwin, Charles—*Origin of Species*, Chapter 6, paragraph 30

In considering the "how" of anything, origin plays a major role in uncovering the mystery of science. When we have an evolutionary mindset, the first time that we contemplate the first birth of the first human baby we find ourselves trying to solve the causality dilemma. Did the first baby arrive from an egg, fertilized by a sperm, but without the mechanism of a human womb or did a full grown human come into being and then fertilize an egg? From here, the natural mind starts looking deeper and deeper into the conundrum until we have the mental equivalent of the proverbial dog chasing his own tail. Evolutionists would like us not to think of the first human birth but would want us to move back the evolutionary tree to perhaps something much more of a simple life form—say, a trilobite[34]. However, as anyone who has studied trilobites will tell you, these were not simple either—nothing living is. As we look at the lowly trilobite[35], we don't see simplicity. What we see is a system of information, complexity, organization and integration. These are all traits of our Lord's Creations. Granted a trilobite is not like us; we are to God, The-Top-Of-The-Line. Like the most expensive car model where all the fancy accessory options come as standard equipment, we are "fully loaded." We can truly boast in our Jesus Christ that we are above all the creatures. Nevertheless, the trilobite's "standard equipment" package is incredible to behold.

VESTIGIAL ORGANS

But what about vestigial organs that claim to be proof that we came from other species? Vestigial organs are supposed to be organs found in the human body that evolutionists claim have no purpose today

---

[34] any of numerous extinct Paleozoic marine arthropods (group Trilobita) having the segments of the body divided by furrows on the dorsal surface into three lobes – Merriam Webster

[35] I only call the trilobite lowly to make a point. God's design and complexity is visible in them, as it is in all things He creates.

and must be left over from a previous ancestor in our evolutionary chain. Some of the organs cited are structures like the appendix[36].

Don't these organs without a known purpose indicate some kind of transition of the human species? NO. As late as 1960, some of America's school textbooks listed over 200 vestigial organs in the human body. This is information that was being packaged and fed to schoolchildren in support of the government's politically correct view of how we all came to inhabit "Mother Earth." Today, we know the purpose of everyone of those vestigial organs listed in the 1960 textbooks. This is simply a case of science playing catch-up with God's Word. Consider the scripture: *But you, Daniel, close up and seal the words of the scroll until the time of the end.* **Many will go here and there to increase knowledge.**" *Dan 12:4 (NIV)* Did I mention that two of the vestigial organs on the 1960's list were the pituitary and the thyroid glands? I guess God was right when He said that if we went "here and there", knowledge would increase, but the whole process seems to be taking too long to my way of thinking.

MATHEMATICS

But what about …? Oh no, here comes more "vain babblings" from the evolutionists. What if evolution were taking place right before our eyes at such a slow pace that we could not observe or detect it? Moreover, supposing the earth is so old that we could claim that piece-meal changes have had enough time[37] to accomplish these evolutionary feats. This is the classical argument that if we have **enough** monkeys striking the keys of **enough** typewriters for **enough** time, one of them would be able to type the complete text of a Shakespearean play. At the onset of the theory of evolution they asked us to believe that the earth was 4 billion years old. They were satisfied this timeframe gave piece-meal, non-goal oriented evolution

---

36 Long regarded as a vestigial organ with no function in the human body, the appendix is now thought to be one of the sites where immune responses are initiated.

37 To evolutionary thinking, Time is always the Hero—With enough time, anything can happen.

ample time to perform its molecule-to-man fairy tale. As our math got better, they pushed the figure for the universe to 7 billion. Today, they've asked for a figure of 17 billion. In order to help them with their argument, I want them to have 30 billion years. (The earth is not that old but we'll deal with that later.) First, let's get a handle for dealing with some of these huge numbers we'll be using.

We'll begin with a very small number—say 1 trillion. So that I don't have to waste a lot of paper typing and you don't have to read a string of zeros, let's convert these calculations to cardinal[38] numbers with exponents. Thus, a million becomes 10^6, a billion—10^9, a trillion—10^{12}, and so on. Now let's see the significance of change when we add exponents. Suppose you and I started a business with an initial capital reserve of $1 trillion. Let's say we weren't very good at business and on the first day, we lost 1 million dollars, and then continued that rate of loss seven days a week, 52 weeks a year. By losing 1 million dollars every day we are in business, how long will it take us to lose 1 trillion dollars? Are you ready? At this rate of loss, it would take over 2,700 years to lose our original nest egg of $1 trillion. That's right. If we had started in business 700 years before Cleopatra met Mark Anthony, it would have taken us until 1997 to lose 1 trillion dollars. Therefore, you can see that 10^{12}, a trillion, is quite a bit bigger than 10^6, a million. What I'd like you to see is that just a small increase in the exponents (in this example from an e6 to e12), makes a huge difference in the quantity. (A billion is a thousand million—a trillion, a thousand billion.)

Now let's get to the big numbers. In 1 billion years, there are 10^{17} seconds[39] and the universe is estimated to contain 10^{80} electrons. If we try to form a single protein by making a million tries a second for 30 billion years and using all the electrons of the universe, can we randomly produce a man? This sounds just like our monkeys pecking away at their efforts to reproduce a Shakespearean play,

---

38   Cardinal numbers are numbers that express a quantity or value as opposed to an ordinal number which express a position i.e. 1st, 2nd, 3rd and so forth.

39   More accurately 3.15576 x 10^16 seconds—For a simplicity, it was rounded to 10^{17}.

doesn't it? I have the calculations in an earlier paper and won't repeat them here but for those that have an interest in this area, I would refer you to the works of R.L. Wysong.[40] He calculated the probability of forming the proteins and DNA for the smallest self-replicating entity would be 1 chance in $10^{167,626}$. When you compare this huge number to the number of estimated electrons in the universe, 10^{80}, you see the enormous implications. Even at this, we would only have a replicating protein—not a man (don't forget the time required to develop a human eye). Here's the kicker. Mathematicians give any chance greater than 1 in 10^{50} as having a zero probability[41]. We have 1 in $10^{167,626}$. **Today, few mathematicians worth their salt give evolution even the slightest chance of success – it has a zero probability.** No, Virginia, a typing pool consisting of monkeys cannot reproduce a Shakespearean play – I don't care how big the typing pool is. The creative process requires intelligent, well-planned forethought. Thank you God for carefully planning when you made me.

RADIOMETRIC DATING

Let's now turn our attention to the age of the universe. But isn't that a simple matter? Couldn't we just date the oldest rocks using the most modern radiometric dating methods and have a pretty good idea how old the universe is? NO. Let's start by looking at one of the great prophecies of the Bible. *First of all, you must understand that in the last days scoffers will come, scoffing and following their own evil desires. They will say, "Where is this 'coming' he promised? **"Ever since our fathers died, everything goes on as it has since the beginning of creation."** 2 Peter 3:3-4 (NIV)* When considering the age of the earth we must start with the field of science called geology. In the early days of this field, geologists were frustrated with their attempts to estimate the age of the earth because of the interruption of the Great Flood. They all believed that sometime after creation there was

---

[40] Wysong, R.L., *The Creation-Evolution Controversy*, Inquiry Press, Midland, Michigan, 1981, p 117

[41] The Collapse of Evolution, Third Edition 2006 by Scott M. Huse, page 123

a catastrophic calamity, Noah's Flood, and this altered the earth's condition to the point where it was difficult to perform any kind of linear calculations on the age of the earth. Not to worry—science came to the rescue. In 1795, a Scottish geologist by the name of James Hutton came along and presented his paper, "The Theory of the Earth." His paper eliminated the idea of a great flood and he was able to unequivocally announce to the world, *"Ever since our fathers died, everything goes on as it has since the beginning of creation."* This, of course, simplified the math greatly and advanced the science of geology at the same time. The only problem was that no one paid any attention to him—that is, not until Sir Charles Lyell picked up the baton in the mid-19th century and published his *Principles of Geology*. You see what Lyell did that Hutton was unable to do, was to give the idea a name – UNIFORMITARIANISM. What man of science wouldn't like to go around, pipe in hand and leather elbow patches on a tweed jacket, having a word as impressive as this roll off his tongue. UNIFORMITARIANISM! Uniformitarianism is summed up in the belief that the **present** is the **key** to the **past** or as God's Word states, *"Ever since our fathers died, everything goes on as it has since the beginning of creation."* By the way, Charles Lyell's *Principles of Geology* was to be the most significant contribution to Darwin's *Origin of Species*. Darwin and Lyell were friends but even this friendship did not allow Lyell to swallow the molecule-to-man nonsense Darwin was peddling. But, that's another story. Let's get back to one of my favorite words, UNIFORMITARIANISM.

Now with the record of Noah's Flood expunged from world history (at least from the scientists' viewpoint) there was no interruption to account for interpreting the past and so, man could become an expert on what took place outside of all recorded history by simply looking at things in the present. (Uniformitarianism = the present is the key to the past) Consider the implications to this. It is perhaps the greatest "magic trick" in the history of mankind. Before this we required a recorded history of what had gone on that was beyond our view but now, the past was forced to yield up its secrets because we could simply view the present and know all things. To me the warning of this in the Book of Peter is one of the great, fulfilled prophecies of the Bible and so I want to give it to you again in its entirety.

> [3:1] *This is now the second letter that I am writing to you, beloved. In both of them I am stirring up your sincere mind by way of reminder,* [2] *that you should remember the predictions of the holy prophets and the commandment of the Lord and Savior through your apostles,* [3] *knowing this first of all, that* **scoffers will come in the last days with scoffing**, *following their own sinful desires.* [4] *They will say, "Where is the promise of his coming?* **For ever since the fathers fell asleep, all things are continuing as they were from the beginning of creation."** [5] *For they deliberately overlook this fact, that the heavens existed long ago, and the earth was formed out of water and through water by the word of God,* [6] *and that by means of these the world that then existed was* **deluged with water** *and perished.* [7] *But by the same word the heavens and earth that now exist are stored up for fire, being kept until the day of judgment and destruction of the ungodly. 2 Peter 3:1-7*

Before going into radiometric dating let me give you a simple method of applying uniformitarianism.

This theory says we can calculate the age of a river by 1) estimating the amount of sediment buildup at the mouth of the river ***presently*** and then 2) measure the amount of sediment in a liter of water drawn from the river at the ***present*** time 3) calculate the ***present*** flow-rate (volume) of the river. Using this information we then do a little simple arithmetic and find out the estimated age of the river by calculating how long it would take to create a buildup of sediment equal to what we currently observe at the mouth of the river. Wow! What a science! On the surface it appears to be sound—estimating, measuring and calculating—all the things true science calls for. It's easy to see how simple it is to make these calculations if you can assume that the present is **always** the key to the past. To assume that a river always flowed at the same rate and always carried the identical amount of sediment are huge assumptions. Consider the following application of this nifty bit of scientific application. Suppose I'm in my home when I suddenly go into a deep coma. When I awake exactly two weeks to the minute, I find that I am a passenger in an automobile. I look at my calendar watch and see that I've been out for exactly two weeks. I check the compass heading on the dash and determine the direction of travel. Next, I look at the speedometer to see the rate of speed. Now all I have to do is assume that for two weeks I've been traveling in that direction and at that constant speed. Knowing that we left from my house, I can know exactly where I am. My assumptions must be that the driver of the car never changed speed, or stopped and never altered compass heading for the entire two weeks. Being interested in pure science I would probably carry my calculations out at least six places right of the decimal point. That should prove once and for all what a slave to accuracy I am. Silly you say—that's not science. Then get a load of this one.

There are these rocks and I want to know how old they are. I know that certain elements are unstable and will decay (emit radiation and particles) until it becomes stable. We call this the conversion of "parent" elements into "daughter" elements. If we know the rate of decay of this particular element, we can determine the age of the rock if (and here comes the silly assumptions) we assume 1) the rock started out with only parent elements, 2) no new parent or daughter elements are introduced[42] and 3) the rate of decay was constant. If we can assume all this we can mathematically index the daughter and parent elements, carry our calculations out six places and **voilà**: we know exactly how old the rock is. Wait a minute while I don my tweed jacket with the elbow patches and light up my pipe. It would do just as well to take our rock for a two-week ride in the car.

Allow me to use UNIFORMITARIANISM for just a minute to prove the earth is no older than 10,000 years. Keep in mind, I don't believe in this theory but I want you to see how science sifts through their bank of information to prove their point. If it doesn't support their agenda, the information is simply swept under the proverbial

---

42   This calls for a "closed system", something we don't observe in the field.

rug. Anyway, listen to this. We have been measuring the strength of the earth's magnetic field for over 100 years—longer than almost any other scientific observation. We know that it has a half-life of 1,400 years. That is, 1,400 years in the future the magnetic field will be half as strong as it is today and 1,400 years ago, it was twice as strong as it is now. A little hocus-pocus (the application of UNIFORMITARIANISM) and I assume this rate was always constant. Now if I extrapolate these figures I find that going back 10,000 years the earth would have a magnetic field about the same strength as our strongest magnetic star—about right, I'd think. If I take these figures back 20,000 years, the magnetic current would have been so strong that they would have melted the planet. Not a good thing when you're trying to get started with a new planet.

There were rock samples taken during the Mt. Helens' eruption. These igneous rocks were formed in a single afternoon but the lab report came back that they were millions of years old. For those who have an interest in geology we have multiple links on our website where you can investigate for yourself recorded error after error of rocks that were incredulously dated.

BIG BANG

Come travel with me way, way back to a time before nothing existed, between 12 and 15 billion years ago. All of a sudden out of this nothingness, an explosion, so large, so intense and yes, so DISORGANIZED (explosions are just that), was born into existence. Then, from this mass DISORGANIZATION came a swirling that began to develop into information, complexity, organization and integration[43] and thus the cosmic egg was hatched. Now, what could be simpler than that?

According to Alan Guth, physicist at M.I.T, this is all you have to believe to have faith in this version of the "birth" of the universe.

---

43 These qualities are the attributes of all common systems and evident in all of God's Creation

1. At one time all the potential for a firmament of at least 40 billion galaxies was packed into a point smaller than a single proton

2. That within this "point of potential" there was neither hyper-compressed matter, nor super-dense energy, nor any tangible substance and it was a false vacuum. Through all this coursed a weightless, empty quantum-mechanical probability framework called a scalar field.

3. That when the big bang went off, the universe expanded from a pinpoint to cosmological size in just seconds as it traveled at speeds millions of times the speed of light.

4. That as subatomic particles began to unbuckle from the inexplicable proto-reality, matter and antimatter formed and as they collided they destroyed themselves, disappearing as mysteriously as they came into being. But in all this, a residue of standard matter was preserved in such a way to form our asymmetrical universe.

5. That a microscopic, transparent, empty point in this primordial space-time contained enough potential to create not one, but a 100 million universes.

I don't know about you but right now my faith in the above five points is feeling a little weak in the knees. I'm always amazed when people tell me that they are firm believers in the big bang and then openly admit they have no idea as to what tenets of the big bang form their foundation of belief. It seems to me analogous to someone buying a home over the phone in a strange city. What would you know about the neighborhood or property value?

As I mentioned earlier the CERN project in Switzerland with all its 1,000 smart guys, 9,000 magnets, 17-mile long tunnel and a whole lot of money, is trying to produce a gram of matter (a 5 Cent Nickel weighs about 5 grams). Of course CERN is working at an advantage since gravity, time and the magnetic attraction between atoms have already been provided by God and they really don't have to start from scratch—another free lunch for the mind of man.

In the appendix, I've included additional semi-technical comments relative to the big bang. The simple thing here is to imagine how the big bang created organization from disorganization (an explosion) and reversing the Second Law of Thermodynamics in accomplishing this. Common systems exhibit information, complexity, organization and integration; they don't develop them.

MISSING LINK?

I've reserved this last "rock" to look under because it has become the single most disappointing element of evolutionary thinking. Evolution is a hypothesis built on a hypothesis. That is, Darwin, because of his presupposed hypothesis, stated that through "gradualism" species would evolve upward to more complex species. As evidence for this hypothesis he further hypothesized that the fossil record would demonstrate this evidence. It never did.

Consider the following quote by the late Harvard paleontologist Stephen Jay Gould:

> *The history of most fossil species includes two features particularly inconsistent with gradualism: 1). Stasis. Most species exhibit no directional change during their tenure on earth. They appear in the fossil record looking much the same as when they disappear; Morphological change is usually limited and directionless. 2). Sudden Appearance. In any local area, a species does not arise gradually by the steady transformation of its ancestors; it appears all at once and 'fully formed.'*

Darwin's thought process began with the presuppositional starting point that evolution must be true and therefore, gradualism would be the obvious confirmation of this—the evidence was just the opposite. On the other hand, creationists have as their starting point the Word of God and what we see in the fossil records are species showing up fully formed—Just as the Bible proclaimed. This solves the scientific causality dilemmas we spoke of in an earlier section. (God made the chicken first and the chicken in turn, produced the first egg) Whether it's a human, a trilobite or a plant, the evolutionary model cannot overcome the obstacle of causality dilemma.

Stephen Gould who is quoted above was an evolutionist and it must have pained him to admit that there was absolutely no evidence for the gradualism that was the main foundation for evolution. At this point you might speculate that he fell to his knees and received Jesus Christ as his personal Lord and Savior. But evolutionists are a hardy bunch. Even though he had to abandon gradualism he developed a new conjecture (I do not use the word, theory since his conjecture is built on another hypothesis) that he called, "Punctuated Equlibria" (PE). PE suggests that species evolved faster over a shorter period of time, thereby explaining the huge fossil gaps. Gould suggested no natural mechanism by which this could have occurred, but since he was an atheist he had to explain the fossil record somehow. As you might guess, there has never been even the remotest evidence to substantiate this conjecture either.

Again, if one has as their presuppositional starting point, God' Word and then looks at the science, many wonderful discoveries await. For example when we look at God's record of the worldwide flood and go into the field we would expect to find, *"billions of dead things, buried in rock layers, laid down by water, all over the Earth[44]."* What do we find? *"Billions of dead things, buried in rock layers, laid down by water, all over the Earth."*

In addition, I might add, **all over the earth** includes Mount Everest.

What Science Shouldn't Be

> Good science should be devoted to good observation and experimentation. It should not be committed to a majority-rule mentality. As for you and me, we shouldn't be duped by bad or incomplete science. After all, Tycho Brahae, the

---

44 Quote from AIG's KenHam

great Danish astronomer of the 16th century, counted and cataloged all the stars and declared there were a little more than 2,000. Of course, he died before Galileo rolled out his first model of the telescope. I don't want to believe in a science that is driven by human ego or a majority-rule mentality[45]. I like a science that will never go "out of style". ***Heaven and earth will pass away, but my words will not pass away. Matthew 24:35***

SO, WHAT'S NEXT FOR YOU?

If you're an unbeliever I suggest you check out my God—He's cool. I was an atheist until I was almost 40 and then decided to read the Bible in order to uncover the errors that would validate my beliefs. I made a mistake. I started in the Book of John and ended up on my knees.

But perhaps you're a believer and subscribe to the idea that the "church thing" is a 30-minute event each Sunday and that it need not interfere or inconvenience the way you live your life. Boy have I got some news for you. Jesus is **the** inconvenience to life in this world and you better be prepared to turn your comfort upside down and love the One that loved you first.

I've always believed that surely one of the most difficult situations in all of life is to bury a child. I have friends who have. In most cases their struggle continues some 20 or 30 years after the event. Just knowing what God has sacrificed for me tells me that I am the treasure of His heart. ***"For God so loved the world, that he gave***

---

[45] Currently we are seeing man's view of science being played out in the Global Warming controversy. We've seen groups of individuals skew and expunge data that did not support their side of the argument. Also, both sides continue to tout that their side has the most "experts". In science, Majority does not = TRUTH. In the abortion issue, the pro-choice advocates continue to adjust their definition of LIFE because if we went by the science, abortions would have to be stopped immediately. I challenge you to carefully consider the science before making it any part of your belief system.

his only Son, that whoever believes in him should not perish but have eternal life. John 3:16

THE ONE THAT GAVE HIS DEATH FOR US—COMMANDS THAT WE GIVE OUR LIFE TO HIM

If you have any questions of what living for Christ is to look like, please contact me through our website at http://www.creationmuseumoto.org/index.html. Over the years I've pulled together nearly five pages of scripture that provides snapshots of a life in submission because of the reciprocal love that comes from being loved first by the Creator of the Universe. I'll be glad to forward them to you.

Ron Walser

Epilogue

Try as we may to "put on the mind of Christ", it is impossible for us to grasp all things of the Bible. ***"The secret things belong to the Lord our God, but the things that are revealed belong to us and to our children forever, that we may do all the words of this law. Deuteronomy 29:29*** As this verse in Deuteronomy says, some things are meant to be a mystery to us but the things our God has revealed belong to us and our children forever. With creation references in 62 of the 66 books of the Bible, it has been my goal to expose you, the reader, to a force of scripture like no other in the Bible. God did not intend us to be ignorant with regards to creation and so He provided a repetitious account of His work all through His Word. I pray that if you're still not convinced of the biblical account of creation you will make a continued effort to seek His Voice in this matter.

With regards to apologetics, I started teaching on the subject in the early 80's and the young people coming to my classes taught me a lot. Early on I discovered that nearly all of them had one or more major obstacles that kept them from having the full measure of faith in the Word of God that provides the peace of victory that Christ has promised. The classes were never lecture-driven and we worked hard to create an environment that would encourage attendees to voice the faith-weakening hindrances that caused them concern. Then, as it is today, many find it difficult to approach God's Word as a "little child" and not bring the lessons of the world to the studying of the Bible. The science portion of this book came from a short paper I wrote in 1997 entitled, *The Princess and the Frog* and was the result of a requested recap summarizing subjects we discussed in these sessions.

After twenty-five years of teaching apologetics, I remain committed to the idea that no one can be argued into accepting Jesus Christ as their Lord and Savior. Acceptance of God's offer is still by the conviction of the Holy Spirit and no matter how eloquent we endeavor to become, Faith still comes from hearing and hearing from the Word of God. In that way, we are all saved by the same means—first we are enabled by the Spirit as we are given a new heart and a new spirit (Ezekiel 36:26), then we hear; faith comes; we believe. Nevertheless, I have encountered many young students who have been filled to the brim with so many thoughts of unbelief that they need help in "emptying" out these obstacles before taking in the things of the Kingdom. (Paul refers to this *kenosis* (emptying out) in Philippians 2:5-11.) Whether witnessing or making disciples, I believe it's important to ask what issues make it difficult for an unbeliever or baby Christian to build on their faith. Young people are no different; they need to be asked.

Today, things are much worse. Europe's church attendance is down from 45% to 7%; Scandinavia is at 1 ½%. In America, over 80% of kids raised in Christian homes and attending public schools leave the church after they leave home and church attendance is down everywhere we look. The latest PEW FORUM ON RELIGION AND PUBLIC LIFE[46] found that 57% of attendees at evangelical churches, and 83% of mainline churches, believe there are many ways to salvation. As the issue of Creation many years before, now a majority of those attending church believe that the Cross is irrelevant. Like Europe, we are becoming increasingly humanistic

---

46 **http://religions.pewforum.org/pdf/report2-religious-landscape-study-full.pdf** on page 58

and this generation is selling out to the cultural worldview in huge numbers.

Is there anything today's churches can do to stem the tide in this fight? I believe so. Like most problems, the solution cannot depend on changing one component of what we're doing and expect much impact on the problem. Below is a sequenced outline that touches on much of the infrastructure with regards to how we "do church."

SUGGESTED STEPS TO TAKE

1. Recognize the problem

    a. It is not about a science issue; it's about the authority of scripture. Our defense of the Word must begin at Genesis 1:1 and extend through to Revelation 22:21

2. We need to have a yearlong in-reach program dedicated to getting all the lost attendees of our church saved.

    a. I've heard estimates all the way from 50 to 70% of the church pews are filled with "social Christians" who really are unsaved. The PEW report mentioned above tends to support these high numbers.

3. Have in place a strong BASIC (**B**ible **A**nswers **S**ecured **I**n **C**hrist) TRAINING program for all new believers and transfers from other churches, teaching them in the things that the Christian Church "holds tight in their hand."

    a. ***Matthew 28:19-20 (KJV)*** *[19] Go ye therefore, and teach all nations, baptizing them in the name of the Father, and of the Son, and of the Holy Ghost: [20]* **_Teaching_** *them to observe all things whatsoever I have commanded you: and, lo, I am with you always, even unto the end of the world. Amen.*

4. Work diligently with the male household heads to teach them to once again become the spiritual leaders in their homes.

5. Restructure the children programs in order to counter the effects of what they're being taught by the culture. (The public school, by law, can only teach a naturalistic reason for creation and there can be no hint of a Creator. Additionally, most of what they will see on TV supports the same dogma.)

   a. The approach needs to be divided into three stages.

      i. Elementary Grades –start by working with these ages, explaining a biblical worldview as opposed to what they'll hear from the culture. There are good curriculums available that expose these young students to the "proof" of God's existence.

      ii. Junior High—further prepare this age group to deal with the difficulties they will be encountering in their science classes. i.e. Teach them to answer test questions that conflict with God's Word by saying, *"as taught in class, the answer is. . ."*

      iii. High School—set up open-dialog venues where students are comfortable to air the obstacles that are pressing in on their faith. Have facilitators trained with answers so that they can respond to the issues that are raised. Show DVD's and distribute books that support the biblical view of Creation.

I realize many will say that they are comfortable in their faith and need no special training in any of these areas. That's fine for them but I know from experience that this logic does not apply to everyone and we are commanded to love our neighbors; yes, even when they are different from us.

Ron Walser

Note: *In this appendix that follows I've included some additional examples of God's Fingerprints plus a few quotes by famous people. These brief descriptions are somewhat semi-technical and I must admit, will not appeal to everyone. Nevertheless, I include them for those hardy souls who wish to trudge on. Be sure to sign up for our newsletter which each month highlights God's wonders. Also, at our website,* ***http://www.creationmuseumoto.org/index.html*** *you'll find articles and links to additional sites where I'm sure your appetite for meeting God through exploring His Creation, can be assuaged.*

Appendix

REALLY BIG NUMBERS

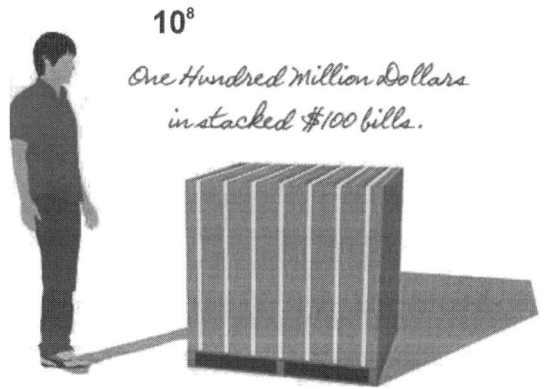

10^8

One Hundred Million Dollars in stacked $100 bills.

Big numbers are hard to get our minds around. They just are. We'll start with some relative small numbers and then move up.

In the figure to the left a man is standing by a pallet of $100 million, all in $100 bills. You can see that that this amount is represented by the scientific notation: 10^8.

Now, looking at the figure below we see $1 trillion, again in $100 bills. You can almost see the man that is standing at the lower left hand corner of the pallets and please note these pallets are stacked two-high.

Again, the above amount as a scientific number is 10^8 – the figure below is 10^{12}. Here you can visualize the huge difference between the two amounts when we only go from an exponent of 8 to 12.

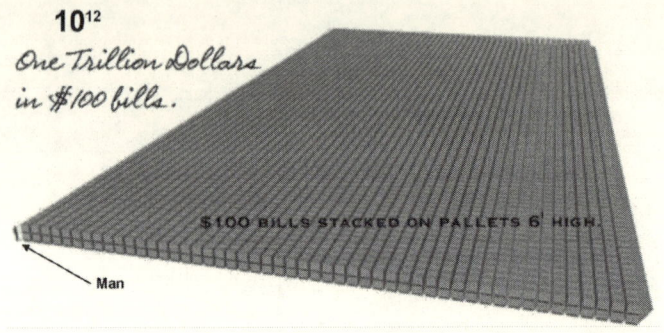

*In 1953 James Watson and Francis Crick discovered the key molecule of life, the DNA—a discovery that earned them the Nobel Prize. Crick, an atheist and an evolutionist, co-Nobel prizewinner with Watson, calculated the probability of a DNA molecule arising spontaneously over the course of the 4.6 billion years to be **ZERO**. (Any odds greater than 1 in 10^{50} is considered to have a zero chance.)*

Crick, an evolutionist to the core, came up with a scenario even more far-fetched than evolution. He called his new brainchild "directed panspermia." Now pan means "all" and spermia means" sperm." His new theory was that an advanced race of beings, living on some far-off planet, sent out space ships with their sperm aboard and seeded various planets. Even a student in elementary school would ask the next obvious question, "How did these advanced beings come into existence?"

Like Crick, Sir Fred Hoyle and the mathematician, Chandra Wickramasinghe, calculated the possibility of an entire cell originating spontaneously in a 15 billion-year-old universe to be 1 in $10^{40,000}$. Again, since anything greater than 1 in 10^{50} is a virtual zero, there is no light *at the end of this tunnel either. Is there any wonder that starting in the mid 80's and continuing today, mathematicians continue to abandon the evolutionary bandwagon. Who wants to believe in something that has a* **ZERO** *chance of happening?*

ASTROPHYSICS

But what about the spacing of the universe, the distances between the stars? Doesn't that prove that the universe is billions of years old? Again, no. From edge to edge, the universe is incredibly large. If it all started from a single point and then expanded at incredible velocity, it would require billions of years to achieve its current proportions. We know this because the speed of light is a constant 300,000 km/sec (186,000 miles / sec) and it would have taken this long for the light of some of the most distant stars to reach us. Additionally, in 1927 Hubble discovered that other galaxies were rushing away from our own at an incredible speed and extrapolating backwards from a central point, estimating the universe to be 2 billion years old. The operative phrase is "central point" and we need to keep that in mind as we explore this line of reasoning. The universe is expanding. The expansion we can observe and that makes the concept of an expanding universe good science. Originally, Einstein based his calculations for the Special Theory of Relativity on a "static" universe (one that was always in existence and stationary) but after Hubble's discovery that the universe was expanding, Einstein proclaimed that it had been the biggest blunder of his life. How did Hubble know the universe was in motion? It is possible to ascertain the movement of sound or light waves, either towards or away from us, by means of the Doppler effect. In the case of sound waves, the waves reaching our ears from an approaching noise compress (shorten) and this causes an increase in pitch. As the noise moves away from us, the waves become elongated and the pitch drops. An example of the phenomena would be the sound of a racecar approaching, and then departing from a fixed point of observation. This shortening and lengthening is the same for light waves and is measurable on a spectrometer. The light waves moving towards us, the ones that are shortened, will be what are called "blue-shifted[47]", those moving away, "red-shifted." So, through good scientific principles of observation we can determine that the universe is dynamic (changing) and not static as once thought. But what about starting from a central point? Science loves this concept. They like to imagine (I'm sorry) "theorize" that the universe had a central starting point where something caused an incredible "big bang" which triggered a pre-existing energy to be converted into mass and this mass, the universe, started hurling away from its origin. (I'll have more to say on the conversion of energy into mass later.) If this dream (I'm sorry) theory were correct, then they are asking for a huge "free lunch." That is, the universe created itself without any help from a god. But God never signed off on the "big bang" and never said the universe started from a central point. In fact, He said just the opposite: *God made two great lights--the greater light to govern the day and the lesser light to govern the night. He also made the stars. God set them in the expanse of the sky to give light on the earth, to govern the day and the night, and to separate light from darkness. And God saw that it was good. Genesis 1:16-18 (NIV)*

God says He didn't form the universe from a central point. But what about the "big bang"? It's so neat. But alas, today the "big bang" is running into trouble. Scientific imaginations and theories come and go but God has said, *"...My words will never pass away."* Since He was the only one that was there at the time, the only eyewitness, then I suppose His account is, was, and will be, the best source, the only source worth listening to. But why is the "big bang" starting to fizzle?

"Everywhere in the universe, galaxies and stars and atoms are observed in roughly the same proportion, and the background radiation is remarkably uniform. Parts of the sky on opposite sides of the visible universe, however, are so far apart that light has not had time to travel between them. The question then arises: If different parts of the sky have never been in contact, how did they become so uniform? In addition, the big bang fails to account for the clumpiness

---

47 Although most of the universe is expanding away from us, some of the galaxies are blue-shifted (moving towards us).

now seen in the universe. That is, while different parts of the universe look roughly the same, they are also speckled with stars and galaxies and other objects. If the big bang produced a homogeneous universe, how did such lumpiness develop? Where did the initial density fluctuations come from that could have seeded the growth of such large conglomerations of mass?

"Finally, the big bang fails to account for the present overall shape of the universe. If the universe had been even slightly convex, with positive curvature (curled inward), at the beginning, it would have quickly collapsed. If it had been even slightly concave, this outward curvature would have become so exaggerated that the universe would have immediately flown apart. This implies that the universe started out completely flat. How did it get that way?"[48]

LIGHT PROPERTIES[49]

But what about the very start of it all? The creation of the first atom (not Adam), even the creation of time itself. We need to look at some of the properties of light to get even a glimpse into what God meant when He said, "In the beginning…."

Light is a mystery, an enigma that Einstein spent the better part of his life studying. In the end, he left behind more questions than answers. Some have called light the most basic form of energy. Others say that it is not energy at all but a transport for the actual energy – a kind of wave-front that facilitates the delivery of energy. Both the Special and General Theory of Relativity go a long way in describing characteristics of light but don't answer what it is. Einstein

---

48 Grolier Encyclopedia – 1996

49 The discussion that follows here is the phenomena of time dilation. The important issue is that time had to be created and is not fixed. The phenomenon discussed here is from the Special Theory of Relativity and has to do with velocity. There is also a dilation that is postulated to occur with nearby gravitational masses. It is this time dilation that many physicists believe addresses the issue of distant starlight and time problems. For those wishing more detail on this subject I suggest searching "distant starlight problem" on the various apologetic websites.

used earlier experiments of light's constant speed of 300,000 km per second[50] to theorize that if we were to move at speeds approaching this incredible velocity, time would slow down to those in a fixed position relative to the movement of the light. i.e. If we were to leave earth in a rocket ship traveling at a constant speed of 299,999 km / sec and return after 94 days of our time (the passenger's), we would find that 100 years would have elapsed for those on earth. If we travel at the same rate of speed as light, time stops altogether.[51] But why should this mystery be of interest or concern to Christians? Let's look at the Bible.

In the first five verses of Genesis we find: *1 In the beginning God created the heavens and the earth. 2 Now the earth was formless and empty, darkness was over the surface of the deep, and the Spirit of God was hovering over the waters.3 And God said, "Let there be light," and there was light.4 God saw that the light was good, and he separated the light from the darkness.5 God called the light "day," and the darkness he called "night." And there was evening, and there was morning—the first day.*

So, we see that on the first day God used His Word to create light. (And God **said**). Let's jump to His work on the 4th day.

14 And God said, "Let there be lights in the expanse of the sky to separate the day from the night, and let them serve as signs to mark seasons and days and years, 15 and let them be lights in the expanse of the sky to give light on the earth." And it was so.16 God made two great lights--the greater light to govern the day and the lesser light to govern the night. He also made the stars.17 God set them in the expanse of the sky to give light on the earth,18 to govern the day and the night, and to separate light from darkness. And God saw that it was good.19 And there was evening, and there was morning--the fourth day. Gen 1:14-19 (NIV)

---

50 A mosquito flying at this speed could encircle the earth at the equator 7.5 times in one second.

51 Although we've not been able to travel at speeds even remotely approaching the speed of light, experiments with extremely accurate atomic clocks have been conducted at high speeds and the time differences bear out Einstein's calculations.

Do you see the problem? On day one God, through His Word, created light but it wasn't until the 4th day that He created what we would logically believe to be the source of the light. We have a dilemma. Either God made a mistake in having Moses record the proper sequence of events or something is going on here that we haven't figured out yet. Let's assume for the moment that God knew what He was doing and what He was describing. If light is not actually energy but is in fact, the transport for energy, then it makes sense that before any energy could be used the first time, cosmic light would have to be created. Jesus Christ, the agent of all creation and the creative force of the Trinity, would have to create the energy transport up-front before he could use any energy at all. We know that the creative process was Jesus' role because we read in the first chapter of John: *In the beginning was the **Word**, and the Word was with God, and the Word was God. He was with God in the beginning.* ***Through him all things were made; without him nothing was made that has been made.*** *(John 1: 1-3)*

We see another interesting reference point. John says that in the beginning was "the Word." In Genesis it says that God used the Word to release the power of creation. And God said, "Let there be…" Each time he used the Word in this way, things happened—big things! So how did Jesus accomplish this miracle of creating something out of nothing; a feat that had never happened before that time and has not happened since? Einstein had stated that $E=MC^2$ or that Energy = Mass times the Speed of Light squared. Since the Speed of Light squared is such a big number, it prompted him to add that every gram of material (mass) packs an incredible amount of energy. This was fully realized with the dropping of the atomic bombs at the close of World War II. To get a glimpse of how Jesus reversed this procedure, that is, instead of turning mass into energy He turned energy into mass. We must rebalance the equation. Thus $E=MC^2$ can algebraically be changed into $M=E/C^2$. I say algebraically since it is a simple matter to treat both sides of the equation the same and come up with an equation that moves the Mass to the left side. In application, we have yet to make it work because we can't harness enough energy to fulfill the formula. Looking again at our formula,

$M=E/C^2$, we see that to produce matter we must have enough energy so that it can be divided by the speed of light squared. Since we don't know of a force of this magnitude in the entire universe, we have adopted total trust in the First Law of Thermodynamics or the Law of Conservation of Energy. You probably remember it better from your high school science classes as: "neither energy nor matter can be created or destroyed." I submit that generating this kind of energy is not a problem for Jesus Christ and He can work the above formula frontward and backward, even sideways, whenever He chooses.

There is something else about light. Earlier I said that if we could travel at the speed of light, all time would stop. Maybe the cosmic light of the third verse of Genesis 1 was created so that time could be jumpstarted. God, the Trinity, created a tri-universe—one with space, time and matter. How interesting that light too, is a trinity. Passed through a prism, light will divide into three basic distinct colors: blue, red and yellow. And one last thing: Jesus is said to be the "Light of the World." Could this have added meaning? If light is the transport of all energy, does that mean that Jesus, the creative agent of the Godhead, is the transport for all the energy used in creation? These are only my questions and I share them with you not as biblical evidence, but merely to highlight the attributes of our unfathomable God.

For an illustration of some of the effects of light, I've enclosed two example diagrams[52] in the Appendix. The first demonstrates how two observers would view a single event from different locations. The second is how the passage of time would be different from these contrasted locations[53].

In closing, please consider that no other cosmogony even attempts to describe the origin of the universe. Both ancient paganism and modern naturalism begins with a space/time/matter continuum

---

52 We covered these examples in class. You will probably have to recall the lesson in order to fully understand the diagrams.

53 I've written a template in Microsoft Excel demonstrating the effect various speed changes would make in this phenomenon. If you would like a copy of it, please provide a blank 3.5 floppy disk.

already existing in a state of chaos. Even the "big bang" theory, a hypothesis that is now starting to lose its shine among the scientific community, theorizes that something was made out of nothing and leaves out any discussion of the origin of the space/time/matter continuum. This "free lunch" approach to any scientific explanation of creation is no explanation at all. Relative to the creative process, we see the *effect*. In science, there is a law that states that no "effect" can be greater than its "cause." Since creation was the "first effect", there had to be a "first cause." That cause had to be one that could create the most basic source of energy and be able to work the formula $E=MC^2$ in both directions. I conclude that the FIRST CAUSE was our loving GOD.

TIME RELATIVITY

Below I've included an example of time dilation from the special theory of relativity. I recognize most readers will pass this up but I feel compelled to explain why it fits into this narrative for some. Over the years I've found that stumbling blocks for accepting Christ comes in a lot of forms. One is the distant starlight and time conundrum. Although this example of time dilation is with regards to velocity, (distant starlight is an issue subject to gravity from the general theory), it is still germane to point out that time was created and is not constant but is in fact, subject to the laws of relativity.

In the diagrams on page 75, we have a train traveling at the speed of 240,000 km/sec. Supposing from inside the train, we affixed a flashlight to the floor and directed the beam so that it would travel to a mirror on the ceiling directly above.

If the flashlight were turned on and an observer on a platform next to the track watched the effect for 10 seconds, what would be the outcome? Because light travels at a constant speed of 300,000 km/sec, we know that in 10 seconds the light would have to travel 3,000,000 km (300,000 X 10). Also, we know that the train, moving at 240,000 km/sec, would have traveled 2,400,000 km in this elapsed time (240,000 X 10 = 2,400,000). Since the speed of the train is nearing the speed of light, the stream of light from the flashlight will form an isosceles triangle as viewed from the platform. Looking at the figure #1, you can see that the line ABC must be 3,000,000 km (Speed of Light X 10 sec) and each of the lines AB & BC would have to be half of this or 1,500,000 km. We also know that the line AC is 2,400,000 km (Speed of Train X 10 sec) and lines AD and CD would have to be half of this or 1,200,000 km. To determine the elapsed time for the passengers we must calculate how far the beam of light has to travel to the ceiling mirror and back, then divide that number by the constant speed of light. Looking at figure #1, you can see that this distance is represented by the line DB plus BD (up to the ceiling and back) and that the line ABD forms a right triangle (fig 2). We can now use the Pythagorean theorem[54] to solve the problem. The calculations are worked out in fig #3 and we find that the beam of light for the passengers traveled a total of 1,800,000 km. Since light travels at 300,000 km/sec, the total elapsed time is 6 seconds (1,800,000 / 300,000 = 6). So what took 10 seconds for the platform observers took only 6 seconds for the passengers.

As I said earlier, as the train speeds up the differences become greater. If the train were traveling at 299,999.999999 km/sec, a one-day trip for the passengers would result in 1,000 years of elapsed time for those on the platform. If you speed the train up to match the speed of light, then time stops altogether. For those who would like to experiment with this further, I've written a TIME DIFFERENCE model on *Microsoft Excel*. You can input various train speeds and the computer will calculate the elapsed times from both points of observation. If you'd like a copy of this file, please contact our website.

In conclusion: ***But do not forget this one thing, dear friends: With the Lord a day is like a thousand years, and a thousand years are like a day. 2 Peter 3:8 (NIV)***

---

[54] In a right triangle, the square of the hypotenuse (AB in our diagram) is equal to the sum of the square of the other two sides (BD & AD)

In figure #1 below, the flashlight is affixed to the floor at point D and is aimed at the ceiling mirror (point B). The observer inside the train "sees" the light travel the path of DB and return BD, while the observer on the platform would observe a path of the light from A to B and finally, C (ABC).

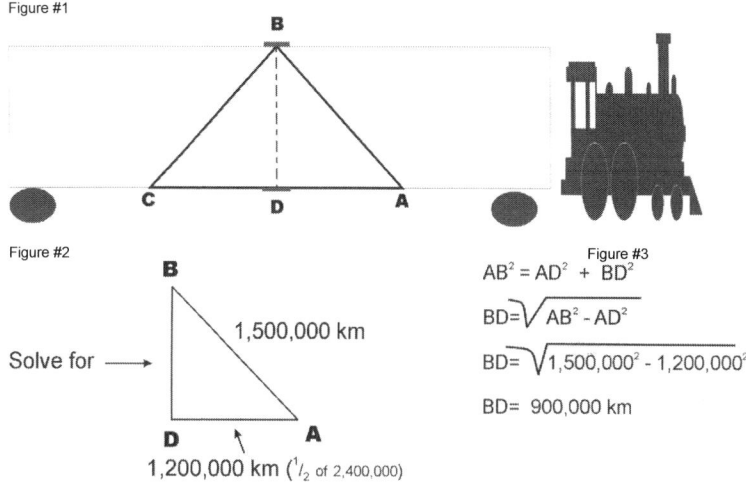

QUOTES—UNFAVORABLE

"Those whose visions dictate that they cannot peacefully coexist with the rest of us, we will have to **quarantine** as best we can. If you insist on teaching your children falsehoods-- that the Earth is flat, that 'Man' is not a product of evolution by natural selection--then you must expect, at the very least, that those of us who have freedom of speech will feel free to describe your teachings as the spreading of falsehoods, and will attempt to demonstrate this to your children at the earliest opportunity. Our future well-being--the well-being of all of us on this planet--depends on the education of our descendants."

Darwin's Dangerous Idea 1996 by Daniel Dennett

"Darwin lives!" said the **Philadelphia Daily News** in an editorial. "The recent ruling by a federal judge that the theory known as *intelligent design* has no place in science classrooms was a stinging slap at the "religious know-nothings" who want to fill our "children's minds with twaddle."

Evolution
Is intelligent design extinct?
1/6/2006

QUOTES—FAVORABLE

My religion consists of a humble admiration of the unlimitable superior who reveals Himself in the slight details we are able to perceive with our frail and feeble minds. That deeply emotional conviction of the presence of a superior reasoning power, which is revealed in the incomprehensible universe, forms my idea of God.

Albert Einstein

"History will ultimately judge neo-Darwinism as a minor twentieth-century religious sect within the sprawling religious persuasion of Anglo-Saxon biology."

Lyn Margulis

Inducted into the World Academy of Art and Science, the **Russian Academy of Natural Sciences**, and the **American Academy of Arts and Sciences** between 1995 and 1998. She is also a proponent and co-developer of the modern version of **Gaia theory**, based on an idea developed by the English atmospheric scientist **James Lovelock**.

Manufactured By: RR Donnelley
Momence, IL USA
July , 2010